The Quotable HARRY S. TRUMAN

"All the beautiful Trumanesque qualities . . . are brilliantly reflected in THE QUOTABLE HARRY S. TRUMAN because it is impossible to read this small, highly readable book without realizing that something he represented, epitomized really, has gone out of almost all public life, though not, as I say, out of American life in general. There is not a page in this book that does not beautifully illustrate what I mean and what is absolutely essential to our future."

—from the Introduction
by Merle Miller

The Quotable Harry S. Truman

Edited by T. S. Settel
& Staff of Quote

With an Introduction by
Merle Miller

A BERKLEY MEDALLION BOOK
PUBLISHED BY
BERKLEY PUBLISHING CORPORATION

Published by arrangement with Droke House, Publishers

Droke House, Publishers
Anderson, South Carolina

Library of Congress Catalog Card Number: 67-13275
SBN 425-02752-X

BERKLEY MEDALLION BOOKS are published by
Berkley Publishing Corporation
200 Madison Avenue
New York, N.Y. 10016

BERKLEY MEDALLION BOOKS ® TM 757,375

Printed in the United States of America

Berkley Medallion Edition, FEBRUARY, 1975

Contents

FOREWORD

"The buck stops here," said Harry S. Truman as he described the awesome responsibilities of the presidency. It was an apt, simple, yet vivid expression of a man who typified the ordinary but did and said extraordinary things. During his term of office and long after, he quipped and quoted and argued in words born of the corn of Missouri and tinged with the hominess of western folk music. Truman's words were not brilliant, nor flowing oratory, not wit nor bursts of the eloquence of Wilson or Kennedy. He said what he meant to say and "there were no two ways about it." He often wrote his own speeches and frequently refused to permit any changes. When necessity required that his speech writers prepare important messages for him, he heavily bluepenciled the material, adding here, subtracting there, providing the essense of his own inimitable personality. And now, in retrospect, after reading his vast number of words, this editor's conclusion can be only a tremendous respect for the former President's good sense and his homey, down-to-earth sagacity which this work reflects.

T. S. SETTEL
Bayside, New York
1967

INTRODUCTION

I did not happen on *The Quotable Harry S. Truman* until some time after I had finished work on *Plain Speaking*. And it is probably just as well; I might have been inhibited in my own writing if I had, although I am pleased to say there are few if indeed any important contradictions between the two books. What is contained in this book is what Mr. Truman said publicly, and *Plain Speaking* has to do almost entirely with what he told me in private. He was better when uninhibited by an audience; he didn't have to spruce up his language for one thing. He never said an off-color word when there were ladies around, and to him all women were ladies. To me he spoke always as a man who had been President, but he also spoke in the language of a man who had commanded Battery D in the First World War.

But it is not surprising that the differences between his public utterances and those in private were so few. The difference between the public man and the private man was almost indistinguishable. He did get fancied up a little in his *Memoirs* and for those speeches some faceless men wrote for him when he first became President, trying to make him sound like Franklin Roosevelt, a hopeless task if ever there was one. In the *Memoirs* other men tried to and in some sad cases succeeded in making him sound like an elder statesman. Thank God that phase didn't last long. As he says in this book, "I hate elder statesmen. I am a Democrat and a politician, and I'm proud of it."

He doesn't say too much in this book about Eisenhower, "the fella that succeeded me in the White House" and one whose name he had the greatest difficulty in pronouncing at all. He does say here that he likes Ike, "but he has gotten mixed up with those damn Republicans and doesn't know which way is up." He also says that generals have no business in the White House, except, perhaps, to pay an occasional visit; as Presidents, never. He mentions General MacArthur only in passing, which is a pity because there were few men in public life about whom he had stronger opinions, most of them negative. He does mention Richard M. Nixon, perhaps not as colorfully as he spoke of him to me. Just before and during the 1960 campaign he said of our Richard, ". . . If he's got any prestige abroad, the country's in a hell of a fix." And later he added, ". . . You don't set a fox to watching the chickens just because he has a lot of experience in the hen house." I sometimes wonder what he would have thought of Watergate and the other incredible things we have learned these last two years. I don't think the fact of it would have surprised him much, but the immense ramifications would have startled and depressed him, as who among us have they not. He once said that whatever the faults and the failures of the men who preceded and succeeded him in the White House, we had never had a corrupt President. I think—and this is second-guessing history, which Harry would have hated—I think he would be dismayed and disappointed, but I don't think he would have lost faith in the system, and he would be right. The system has never seemed stronger than it does at this dark and desperate hour.

Books could and unquestionably will be written about the differences between Harry S. Truman and Richard M. Nixon, but there are really three sentences in this book that say it all; any other words, *lying, deceit, hypocrisy, dishonesty,* all of them simply reinforce what comes under "Optimism" here. And Mr. Truman was always an optimist, always; if he had his bad moments, and he must have, he never admitted them either in public or in private.

> . . . I have grown up to look for the good in people. I have never regarded people with suspicion. Such an attitude usually leads to worry and being a pessimist about everything, people included.

That's it, expressed, as usual, in the unadorned language of truth. Harry Truman never regarded people with suspicion. Do you suppose there is anybody in the world Richard really trusts, ever has? Even Pat, now that she is wearing all those jewels instead of a simple Republican cloth coat?

Harry once said, "I don't have to write down what I say because I always tell the truth." And he did, which often caused him some difficulty as President, particularly with international relations where half-truths or outright lies are, for reasons I have never really understood, or seem to be necessary. As Dean Acheson, Mr. Truman's friend and Secretary of State, has written in his admirable book, *Present at the Creation,* ". . . he was not good in the fast back-and-forth of the press conference. President Truman's mind is not as quick as his tongue. . . . He could not wait for the end of a question before answering it. Not seeing where he was being led, he fell into traps . . . at his press conferences and even more, his early-morning walks followed by inquisitive reporters were a constant menace."

Later Acheson adds, "He learned from mistakes, though he seldom admitted them. That is, he learned from all mistakes but one—the fast answer in that nightmare of Presidents, the press conference. We kept on hand, as a sort of first-aid kit, a boxful of 'clarifications' for these events."

As a result Harry had more than a few quarrels with the press, but he never threatened or even hinted at any kind of censorship. He never thought that his power as President included telling newspaper publishers or heads of networks what they should or should not say about him and his administration. And he would never have thought of looking for a refugee from Disneyland who without laughing or crying or both could say of an outright lie simply that it had become "inoperative."

Harry just once in a while said that after he got out of the White House he might have to punch a few newspaper men in the nose, and he also said that the only good thing the late Senator Joseph McCarthy did was when he knocked down Drew Pearson. Usually, incidentally, it wasn't what newspaper men said about him personally that made him angry. He couldn't and wouldn't allow any attacks or catty (à la Clare Booth Luce) remarks about Bess or Margaret. And there was, of course, the letter he wrote to the music critic of the *Washington Post* who didn't think Margaret's singing voice was much of a threat to the young Maria Callas.

But he was never more eloquent than in his final press conference at the White House, paying tribute to the men who had covered and hounded and hated and loved him for so long. He said:

I think it is important for our democratic system of government that every medium of communication between the citizens and their government, particularly the President, be kept open as far as possible.

This kind of news conference where reporters can ask any question they can dream up—directly of the President of the United States—illustrates how strong and how vital our democracy is. There is no other country in the world where the chief of state submits to such unlimited questioning.

Perhaps succeeding Presidents will be able to figure out improvements and safeguards in the procedure. I hope they will never cut out the direct line of communication between themselves and the people.

Of course television wasn't quite the numbing force it is today when Harry ran for re-election in 1948. But it was around, and there was talk among the Democrats of having a few coast-to-coast television extravaganzas. There weren't any, though. Hell, they had trouble enough getting up fifty thousand dollars for what was then the traditional Labor Day speech from Cadillac Square in Detroit that launched the Presidential campaign. And that was just radio.

And they often had difficulty raising money to pay the way for the campaign train to get from city to city. It looked for a time as if it might be permanently stalled in Oklahoma City, but then Eddie Jacobsen, Harry's partner in failure in the haberdashery, called up some influential and well-to-do friends, most of them Jewish, and they came through with money. Money which not only helped finish that trip, but helped, in large part, to make a second trip possible. The Jews had not forgotten that Harry had a little something to do with the formation of the state of Israel, an act some people said was political, but it was an act dictated by Mr. Truman's heart and from his familiarity with what had happened to the Jews during the Third Reich and throughout most of history.

Indeed after the 1948 election and a year after the birth of Israel the Chief Rabbi came to see the President and told him, "God put you in your mother's womb so that you could be the instrument to bring about the rebirth of Israel after two thousand years."

The statement was perhaps a little extravagant, but it made Harry cry like a baby. And who except God knows? Maybe that's the way it was.

I should add that in 1948 and in all his other campaigns—he once spent a total of $5,000 in a Senatorial election and won—Mr. Truman always wanted to know where the money came from. And if he didn't like the people who wanted to donate it, he wouldn't take it. Nothing personal, you understand; he just didn't like what they stood for and what they thought they were buying. He knew that very few people give money in political campaigns out of sheer goodness of heart.

By the way, during the 1948 campaign trip, the Trumans, all three of them, brought along their own food. Their particular car, the Ferdinand Magellan, had been a gift to Franklin Roosevelt. So, according to J. B. West in *Upstairs at the White House,* ". . . all the Trumans had to pay for was the railroad tickets." Which they did, not us taxpayers.

An extraordinarily perceptive—to me anyway—reviewer said in *Variety* of *Plain Speaking:*

> The 33rd President of the United States did not look on politics as a form of show biz. He eschewed being "an

actor" and the "powder and paint." He met the people eyeball-to-eyeball, gave it to them straight, and they responded. It is possible that Truman's way is the way to turn the whole political scene around so that it will serve the people, as it should.

Congress may have to pass a law making it mandatory that before anyone run for any office above dog-catcher, he must read *Plain Speaking* and prove an understanding of it monitored by Diogenes. While it might be tough to enroll him, it's also tough to find anyone else qualified to referee the event.

That is the way to do it, you know; a Presidential candidate, all candidates for any office must meet the people eyeball-to-eyeball. That's why these candidates for lesser offices, governors and Congressmen and the like, are having such success with their walking tours across districts and states. Some of them don't spend any money on television at all, and they've been winning. There wasn't much magic in the 1972 Presidential campaign, but there was a day in Boston when George McGovern was there himself, on the streets, in the shopping centers and department stores, on steps and curbstones, all over the city, among the people, hundreds of thousands, maybe millions of them. Right there, a real man, not a motion picture, not a shadow on a 21-inch screen, a man shaking hands and greeting the people eyeball-to-eyeball. It was a beautiful and exciting day. I'm not sure that's the reason McGovern carried Massachusetts, but I'm certain it didn't lose him a single vote.

Isn't it ironic? In the early days people used to say of television, even people who didn't get paid for it, that the scrutinizing eye of a television camera would reveal a man's inner character, would bare his soul, if any, to the watching world. There were times—we all have our weaker moments—when I thought and said that myself.

Old Harry had the right idea. He said, "I've got other things to do besides watch television. I never look at it unless my daughter is on

All these beautiful Trumanesque qualities I've been mentioning—and I think there are still a lot of them around, although not visibly in politics at the moment—are brilliantly reflected in *The Quotable Harry S. Truman* because it is impossible to read this small, highly readable book without realizing that something he represented, epitomized really, has gone out of almost all of public life, though not, as I say, out of American life in general. There is not a page in this book that does not brilliantly illustrate what I mean and what is absolutely essential to our future.

For example, take what Mr. Truman said are the necessary qualifications for a man who wants to become President.

> First, he should be an honorable man. Then he should be a man who can get elected. Finally, he should be a man who knows what to do after he is elected.

Simple enough, but that first sentence alone is what is causing us all the trouble these days. "Honorable." "An honorable man." How many times have you heard those words used in a sentence recently? Of how many men in public life today can they be said, without a giggle or a smirk, that is? Who do you think you're kidding? They're all in on the take. They're not, but the ones who are not are depressingly reticent.

Another of the pleasantly surprising things about this book is the way it demonstrates the extraordinary number of ways in which Harry Truman was ahead of his time. Newspaper men missed a lot of it; they didn't pay too much attention to what that flat, dull, often corny man said. They missed the imperial manner and the Harvard-Groton accent of his predecessor. Drew Pearson, who started out by hating Harry Truman and ended up by at least grudgingly admiring him, says in the *Diaries* (1949-1959) of Mr. Truman's early days as President, "Sumner [Welles] pointed to one difference between Truman and F.D.R., which I expect few people realize—namely, the fact that Truman has never read a history book in his life. You can't mold history, according to Sumner, unless you know history."

Sumner Welles was a good, some people even say great, diplomat but he didn't know anything at all about Harry Truman's reading habits; almost nobody did at the time.

Harry once said that he couldn't remember a day in his life since he was about four years old or thereabouts when he hadn't read a book, and most of them were histories and biographies. I would say that he probably did more reading of history than any President of this century, with the possible exception of Woodrow Wilson, and in his battle for the League of Nations Wilson forgot something he surely learned in his reading, that in a republican society arrogance always loses, always.

Harry Truman had read as much history and understood it as well as, this may come as a shock but I think it's true, Thomas Jefferson. I don't think Harry read many novels; that was Bess's department, mostly mysteries, and I am told in Independence that she still drives to the library once every week to get an armload of them. She is 89.

Harry also read widely in philosophy and poetry. Spinoza was his favorite philosopher, and he was fond of quoting Horace, who also lived in what might mildly be described as a troubled age, 65-8 B.C., a time when public life was corrupt, and nobody believed in anything much. Harry was fond of quoting, "Take the present, the future's no one's affair."

His favorite poet, though, was Byron, and he was also fond of Tennyson, who is not much in style at the moment; Harry admired him because he was so good at predicting the future, something that Harry, as we shall see, excelled in himself.

Mr. Truman says he read all 3,000 books in the Independence Public Library, which I don't doubt, and that he remembered everything he read. I don't know about *everything*, but at seventy-seven, an age when most men's minds are largely befuddled, he remembered more history than I ever knew, and I have always fancied myself as something of an historian.

Also Harry not only remembered what he read; he was marvelously adept at applying it to the problems at hand. It might also be added that he spent more time in the Congressional Library than any legislator of his day; once he checked out 150 volumes at one time.

As for Franklin Roosevelt, I doubt if he ever finished a history book except, possibly, a few about the U.S. Navy. Maybe he got through a few general histories at Groton and Harvard, but even there I'll bet he skipped a lot. He was not a reader, certainly not a great intellect. He was a man who accomplished what he did by manipulating people. He loved it, was very good at it, and changed the history of this country and the world by doing it. Mostly for the better, too.

But he didn't go around bragging about what he'd read, the way Jack Kennedy often did. He learned that in Independence. You didn't win popularity contests by mentioning that you'd read a book, of all things. In those days it was probably okay if you confessed to skimming through the *Police Gazette*, especially the racier parts, and nowadays it's okay to admit thumbing through *Playboy* and all of its questionable successors.

Books, no; they are for women, even the sleaziest of them—books, not women.

Harry kept his language simple, though, and, as I've said, we like a certain grandness in manner in our Presidents. Which is one reason it was nice to have Jack Kennedy in the White House; he was pretty to look at; he had class, and he spoke like a man who'd at least been in the Harvard Yard. It wasn't quite authentic Harvardese, but it was close enough to get by.

So when at his Inaugural Jack Kennedy said, "Ask not what your country can do for you but what you can do for your country," it was headlined all over the place. Editorials were written about its wisdom, and for a while there you couldn't turn on television without Walter Cronkite or one of those types commenting on the beauty of its basic truth. How did he, how did all those brilliant Camelotians, ever think of it?

Actually, old Harry had said pretty much the same thing during the campaign that nobody but he and maybe Bess thought he could win. It was down in Raleigh, North Carolina, and Mr. Truman said,

> . . . The strength of this Republic lies in the fact that so many millions of men and women, who hold no office and aspire to none, recognize as clearly as Presidents Jackson, Polk, and Johnson [Andrew, not Lyndon B.] did that they must serve their country before they thought of themselves.

Homelier perhaps, but really the same thing isn't it? As a consultant for the Center for the Study of Democratic Institutions recently wrote in the Center's magazine, "One recurring theme in Harry's Presidency was his old-fashioned and rather appealing distrust of designated experts. He was the last President, it seems, who was always on guard against the generals, officials, and bright young men in whom his successors were to place such trust. But it was experts as a caste he suspected rather than expertise. When, through trial and error, he discovered men with a special wisdom, like George Marshall and Dean Acheson, he exploited them unmercifully. On the reverse side of Truman's skepticism of titled authorities was a belief in the mental and moral competence of the people—that is, provided they were dealt with honestly by their leaders. He shared Lincoln's patient confidence in the ultimate justice of the people. Like Lincoln, he spoke in simple unequivocal language, as if he were addressing his neighbors down the street in Independence, Missouri."

Also at Raleigh in that same speech Harry said,

> . . . It takes courage to face a duelist with a pistol, and it takes courage to face a British general with an army. But it takes still greater and far higher courage to face friends with a grievance. The bravest thing Andrew Jackson ever did was to stand up and tell his own people to their own faces that they were wrong.

Harry risked telling most of the people of the United States that they were wrong, oh, numerous times, but, just for example, when he fired General MacArthur, maybe the most popular general since George Washington. Can you imagine any of his successors facing up to such an act? Dick Nixon never could decide what to do about little Lieutenant Calley? Not enough polls on what would be the most popular choice.

Harry never doubted that when he did what had to be done, what was right, the people would eventually go along, and they almost always did. George Gallup has said, "We have accumulated a mountain of evidence by now on how the American people actually felt about the major issues of the last twenty years. . . . Looking back . . . it is possible to say that the judgment of the people has often been wiser than the judgment of Congress, or even of the *experts*." (The emphasis is mine.)

Oh, Harry Truman was ahead of his time all right. About World Government, for instance; he returned again and again to the theme that the peace of the world could not be kept unless there was an international law and an international police force to see that that law was adhered to.

Again, in the ineptly reported campaign of 1948, he said,

> I know that we can get peace in the world if we are in a position to enforce that peace. We wouldn't have peace here in Washington if you didn't have the police around the corner. . . . I am asking for what amounts fundamentally to a police force . . . which will keep the peace in the world.

And Civil Rights? Why, way back in 1940 when he was running for re-election to the Senate, another race nobody thought he could win, he made a civil rights speech advocating measures that even now, a third of a century later, haven't been carried out. It was down in the center of Missouri, not exactly a leader among states in which the citizens are for civil rights, and there wasn't a black face in the audience, mostly rednecks.

Of course a lot of Harry Truman's ideas didn't become law; they weren't even seriously discussed much of the time, but that happens to all Presidents. And Norman Thomas, who never did become President, suggested a lot of ideas that when sanity and integrity return to our government, and they will, will become laws of the land. And the same can be said of a lot of Harry's ideas. Ahead of his time. You bet. By decades, centuries maybe. He knew there had to be World Government because his great friend—many figures of history were like personal friends—Henry IV of France, Henry of Navarre (1572-1610) said World Government was the only answer to world peace, and he was a wise man and was right. It's just that these things take time.

Harry was never threatened by the youth either. He preferred short hair on a young man, but if young people wanted to wear it long, so be it. Privacy and the sanctity of a person's opinion, no matter on what, were close to being sacred to him. Each to his own taste. ". . . Our young people know a great deal more about everything than the people who are criticizing them."

And so on and so on. Mr. Truman's first cousin, Miss Ethel Noland, said that he was a nineteenth century man, which is true enough, but he understood more and did more about the twentieth century than anybody we've had around lately. He was speaking about ecology as far back as 1947; only then, of course, he called it "conservation."

> Conservation has been practiced for many decades and preached for many more. Yet only in recent years has it become plain that we cannot afford to conserve in a haphazard or piecemeal manner. No part of our conservation can be slighted if we want to make full use of our resources and have full protection against future emergencies.

Harry Truman was an elemental man, but he was also one of the most complex men I have ever encountered. The two are not mutually exclusive. It has always been my private theory that

Harry put on the Rotarian manner as a clever camouflage. If you both read books *and* played the piano in those days in Independence, you had to do something to avoid being run or ridiculed out of town.

As I've said elsewhere, Harry was also marvelously adept at applying what he had read to the problem at hand. He was a man who was able to and did make decisions. According to Dean Acheson all he ever asked was, "How long have I got?" He would take what time was available and then decide, and General Marshall, I think rightly, has called this capacity the rarest gift given to man and often repeated that Harry Truman had it to a high degree.

And once the decision was made, Harry stopped worrying about it. That crucial November night in 1948, for instance, knowing the outcome of the election, Mr. Truman says, ". . . I had my sandwich and buttermilk and went to bed at six-thirty." He didn't take a sleeping pill either; I doubt if in his entire life Harry Truman ever took a sleeping pill; men who have done what is right all day seldom need one.

Despite the simplistic exterior, Harry S. Truman was not an easy man to sum up; as I say, he was complicated. Richard Rovere, perhaps the most sophisticated and certainly one of the best Washington correspondents, once wrote of one of Harry Truman's favorite characters in all of history, Marcus Aurelius (Emperor Marcus Aurelius Antoninus—Harry always insisted that I get the entire name right), "he [Marcus, that is] reigned, according to Gibbon, in the period in the history of the world during which the condition of the human race was most happy and prosperous. The vast extent of the Roman Empire was governed by absolute power, under the guidance of virtue and wisdom. The armies were restrained by four successive emperors, whose characters and authority commanded involuntary respect . . . who delighted in the image of liberty and were pleased with considering themselves the accountable ministers of the law. Marcus Aurelius 'was severe to himself, indulgent to the imperfections of others, just and beneficent to all mankind.' "

There is more, much more in the *Meditations* which Marcus Aurelius wrote on the banks of the Danube in a war he detested, as he detested all wars; in the end the severity of the winter proved fatal to the great man. He wrote:

> Make for thyself a definition or description of the thing which is presented to thee, so as to see distinctly what kind of thing it is in its substance, in its nudity, in its complete entirety, and tell thyself its proper name, and the names of the things of which it has been compounded and into which it will be resolved. For nothing is so productive of elevation of mind as to be able to examine methodically and truly every object which is presented to thee in life, and always to look at things so as to see at the same time what kind of universe this is, and what kind of use everything performs in it, and what value everything has with reference to the whole, and what with reference to man, who is a citizen of the highest city, of which all other cities are like families; what each thing is and of what it is composed, and how long it is the nature of this thing to endure which now makes an impression on me.

There is nothing in that paragraph that Harry Truman could possibly have disagreed with, and he was, God knows, ". . . severe to himself, indulgent to the imperfections of others, just and beneficent to all mankind."

After Harry left the White House he was offered all kinds of jobs, none of them for a digit less than six figures a year. High six figures, too. But he turned them all down. Those people weren't interested in hiring him; they wanted to make use of the power of the name of an ex-President. Harry said he'd rather die in the poorhouse than have any part of any of that. As my old friend, a man I have admired for decades now, wrote in the *Baltimore Sun*, "To some, no doubt, that will seem the utterance of a fantastic fool. But in the murky light of Watergate how it shines—how it shines."

That was written by Gerald W. Johnson, and Baltimore could use a few more like him, quite a few, and we have to get Diogenes back for those tests. It won't be easy, but it can be done, and it will. You won't learn all about Harry S. Truman from reading this book, and even after reading *Plain Speaking*, in which I have a very personal interest, you will still want to know more about one of the most remarkable men our country has ever produced. But don't worry; we'll do it again.

And this sentence of Harry's might be as good a way to end as any.

> The ills of society spread like a contagion and no one is safe, but we may take hope in the fact that the good in society is also contagious.

Keep that in mind on the gloomy days.

Merle Miller
Brewster, New York
1974

QUOTATIONS

A

ACTION

. . . We must remember that the test of our religious principles lies not just in what we say, not only in our prayers, not even in living blameless personal lives—but in what we do for others. [1

Address, Washington Pilgrimage of American Churchmen
Washington, D.C.
September 28, 1951

ADVICE

. . . I have had enough experience in all my years, and have read enough of the past, to know that advice to grandchildren is usually wasted. If the second and third generations *could* profit by the experience of the first generation, we would not be having some of the troubles we have today. [2

Statement, 1960

AGRICULTURE

. . . I know of no one factor more important to the future peace of the world than food. The work which FAO (UN's Food & Agriculture Organization) does, or leaves undone, will have a great bearing on the history of the world. [3

Statement
December 1948

. . . One of the great lessons of history is that no nation can be stronger than its agriculture. Hungry and ill-nourished people cannot practice the art of democratic government and peaceful commerce. Peace cannot be built on a foundation of human want. [4

Address
Kansas City
June 7, 1947

ALLIES

. . . Our allies are the millions who hunger and thirst after righteousness. [5

Inaugural Address
January 20, 1949

. . . Some of those that could not defend themselves against invasion have grown vain and inflated and are now turning their backs on us. It is not a pretty picture where those whom we have helped to rescue only yesterday are now deliberately trying to do us harm. [6

Statement
February 1965

. . . America was not built on fear. America was built on courage, on imagination and an unbeatable determination to do the job at hand. [7

Special Message to Congress
January 8, 1947

. . . In our countries we do not measure our prosperity by the power of the state. We do not measure the progress of our society in terms of military might. We do not measure our advancement in terms of the profits or the luxuries of the few. Our yardstick is the welfare of the many. We think in terms of the average man—how he lives, what he can buy, and the freedom he enjoys. These are the standards by which we measure our development. [8

Address, Meeting of
Foreign Ministers of
American Republics
Washington, D.C.
March 26, 1951

. . . Our country is not merely the sum of its parts. It is not the total of its resources, the aggregate of its wealth. Our country is much more than the complement of all our states and boundaries, our cities and our farms. It is the sum of its culture, its heritage, its traditions. It is the sum of its strength, its vigor, and its spirit. [9

Radio Remarks
January 30, 1946

. . . This nation is no wiser than the education of its citizens.

This nation is no stronger than the health of its citizens. This nation's security begins with the welfare of its citizens. [10

Address
Indianapolis
October 15, 1948

. . . Today, America has become one of the most powerful forces for good on earth. We must keep it so. We have achieved a world leadership which does not depend solely upon our military and naval might. We have learned to fight with other nations in common defense of our freedom. We must now learn to live with other nations for our mutual good. We must learn to trade more with other nations so that there may be—for our mutual advantage—increased production, increased employment and better standards of living throughout the world. May we Americans all live up to our glorious heritage. In this way, America may well lead the world to peace and prosperity. [11

Address
Joint Session of Congress
April 16, 1945

. . . **Americans.** The little fellow is the backbone of this country. [12

Statement
September 18, 1949

. . . **Americans.** Because our freedom is in danger we are united to its defense. Let no aggressor think we are divided. Our great strength is the loyalty and fellowship of a free people. We pull together when we are in trouble, and we do it by our own choice, not out of fear, but out of love for the great values of our American life, that we all have a share in. [13

Radio and Television Report
December 15, 1950

. . . **Aspirations.** We have this America not because we are of a particular faith, not because our ancestors sailed from a particular foreign port. We have our America because of our common aspiration to remain free and our determined purpose to achieve for ourselves, and for our children, a more abundant life in keeping with our highest ideals. [14

Address
Columbus, Ohio
March 6, 1946

. . .**Creed.** You know that being an American is more than a matter of where you or your parents came from. It is a belief that all men are created free and equal and that everyone deserves an even break. It is a respect for the dignity of men and women without regard to race, creed, or color. That is our creed. [15

Informal Remarks in
Indiana and Ohio
October 26, 1948

. . . **Faith.** When the United States was established, its coins bore witness to the American faith in a benevolent deity. The motto then was "In God We Trust." That is still our motto and we, as a people, still place our firm trust in God. [16

Radio Address
October 30, 1949

. . . **Forces of Evil.** Racial and religious oppression—big business domination—inflation—these forces must be stopped and driven back while there is yet time. [17

Address in the Chicago Stadium
October 25, 1948

. . . **Good Society.** The good society we are seeking is based on order and peaceful cooperation, among men who share common ideals of freedom and justice. All these things are not easy to attain. For a society is made up of men, who are often weak, and selfish, and quarrelsome. And yet, men are the children of God. Men have within them the Divine spark that can lead them to truth, and unselfishness, and courage to do the right. Men can build a good society, if they follow the will of the Lord. Our great Nation was founded on this faith. Our Constitution and all our finest traditions rest on a moral basis. [18

Address in Spokane, Washington
May 11, 1950

. . . **Image.** America has long been a symbol of freedom and democratic progress to peoples less favored than we have been. We must maintain their belief in us by our policies and our acts. [19

Message to the Congress
February 5, 1947

. . . **Posterity.** We owe to future generations the bequest of a strong America, mighty in its resources and wise in its use of them. We are firmly determined to leave after us a land that is better than we found it. [20

Remarks
Iowa City, Iowa
September 18, 1948

. . . **Responsibilities.** To meet the responsibilities placed upon us today this nation must be strong. A strong United States means a country that maintains a military power commensurate with its responsibilities. It means a country of sound domestic economy. It means a country that holds its place in the forefront of industrial production and continues its leadership in creating the techniques of abundance. It means, most of all, a strong, united, confident people, clear in the knowledge of their country's destiny, unshaken and unshakable in their resolve to live in a world of free peoples at peace. [21

Address
Jefferson Day Dinner
Washington, April 5, 1947

. . . **Rights.** America is dedicated to the conviction that all people are entitled by the gift of God to equal rights and freedoms even though they may differ in religious persuasion, in social and political views, or in racial origin. Our greatness is and will be measured by the degree of our recognition of this fundamental truth. [22

Letter to John L. Sullivan
Accepting the Honorary Chairmanship of National Brotherhood Week
October 5, 1949

. . . **Strength.** We are strong because of many things: our natural resources which we have so diligently developed; our great farms and mines, our factories, shipyards and industries which we have so energetically created and operated. But above all else, we are strong because of the courage and vigor and skill of a liberty loving people who are determined that this nation shall remain forever free. [23

Address
Joint Session of Congress
October 23, 1945

. . . **World Leadership.** With our strength comes a grave responsibility. With it must also come a continuing sense of leadership in the world for justice and peace. [24

Address, Joint Session of the Congress
October 23, 1945

. . . **World Responsibility.** We cannot escape the responsibility which is thrust upon us. What we think, plan, say, and do is of profound significance to the future of every corner of the world. [25

State of the Union Message
January 21, 1946

AMERICANISM

. . . Americanism is not embodied in any one man. It is a distillation of the spirits of all the heroes who have labored and fought and died for the common good. [26

Address
Raleigh, North Carolina
October 19, 1948

. . . We are a diverse people, and in this diversity we have great strength. We have room for differences and room for disagreement. Part of our respect for the dignity of the human being is the respect for his right to be different. That means different in background, different in his beliefs, different in his customs, different in his name, and different in his religion. That is true Americanism; that is true democracy. It is the source of our strength. It is the basis of our faith in the future. It is our hope, and it is the hope of the world. [27

Address, Chicago
Swedish Pioneer Cen-
tennial Association
June 4, 1948

. . . I think it was my predecessor who said that Americanism is not a matter of race or creed, it is a matter of the heart. [28

Remarks
July 15, 1946

APPEASEMENT

. . . If the history of the 1930's teaches us anything, it is that appeasement of dictators is the sure road to world war. If aggression were allowed to succeed in Korea, it would be an open invitation to new acts of aggression elsewhere. [29

Radio and Television Report
September 1, 1950

. . . We are willing to negotiate differences, but we will not yield to aggression. Appeasement of evil is not the road to peace. [30

Radio and Television Report
December 15, 1950

ARMS CONTROL

. . . **Peace.** Two of the greatest obligations undertaken by the United Nations toward the removal of the fear of war remain to be fulfilled. First, we must reach an agreement establishing international controls of atomic energy that will ensure its use for peaceful purposes only. Second, we must reach agreements that will remove the deadly fear of other weapons of mass destruction. Each of these obligations will require the utmost in perseverance and good faith, and we cannot succeed without setting fundamental precedents in the law of nations. Each will be worth everything in perseverance and good faith that we can give to it. The future safety of the United Nations, and of every member nation, depends upon the outcome. [31

Address, New York City, at the
Opening Session of the United
Nations General Assembly
October 23, 1946

ASPIRATIONS

. . . Planning. I was a great admirer of old D. H. Burnham of Chicago, who organized the Chicago regional planning, and he had a motto over his mantel on which was written "MAKE NO LITTLE PLANS." You can always amend a big plan, but you never can expand a little one. I don't believe in little plans. I believe in plans big enough to meet a situation which we can't possibly foresee now. [32

Remarks, American Society of Civil Engineers
November 2, 1949

ATOMIC AGE

. . . Before us now lies a new era in which the power of atomic energy has been released. That age will either be one of complete devastation, or one in which new sources of power will lighten the labors of mankind and increase the standards of living all over the world. [33

Address, Governing Board of the Pan American Union
April 15, 1946

. . . If the civilized world as we know it today is to survive, the gigantic power which man has acquired through atomic energy must be matched by spiritual strength of greater magnitude. All mankind now stands in the doorway to destruction—or upon the threshold of the greatest age in history. Only a high moral standard can master this new power of the universe, and develop it for the common good. [34

Address, Columbus, Ohio
Conference of the Federal Council of Churches
March 6, 1946

ATOMIC BOMB

. . . If a (decision to use the bomb) had to be made for the welfare of the United States and the democracies of the world, I wouldn't hesitate to make it again. [35

Statement
April 10, 1949

. . . There is at least one defense against the atomic bomb. That defense lies in our mastering this science of human relationships all over the world. It is the defense of tolerance and of understanding, of intelligence and thoughtfulness. [36

Address, Fordham University
New York City
May 11, 1946

. . . **Control.** We have offered to surrender the most powerful thing we have under our control, if the world will come in and set up a control of that weapon which will prevent its use for the destruction of mankind. [37

Remarks to new Democratic Senators and Representatives
April 6, 1949

. . . **Use of.** As President of the United States, I had the fateful responsibility of deciding whether or not to use the atom bomb for the first time. It was the hardest decision I ever had to make. But the President cannot duck hard problems—he cannot pass the buck. I made the decision after discussions with the ablest men in our government, and after long and prayerful consideration. I decided that the bomb should be used in order to end the war quickly and save countless lives—Japanese as well as American. But I resolved then and there to do everything I could to see that this awesome discovery was turned into a force for peace and the advancement of mankind. Since then, it has been my constant aim to prevent its use for war and to hasten its use for peace. [38

Address
Milwaukee, Wisconsin
October 14, 1948

ATOMIC CONTROL

. . . Our national policy has been that atomic energy is such a vast new force in our lives that it must be kept under public control as long as the safety of the people's interest require. We must continue to follow that policy. That is the only way we can assure the development of atomic energy for the benefit of humanity. [39

Address
Milwaukee, Wisconsin
October 14, 1948

ATOMIC ENERGY

. . . One of the most earth-shaking discoveries in the history of the world was made—the development of atomic energy was discovered. That discovery was used in the last war effort against Japan, and the effect of that atomic bomb is too terrible for contemplation. But we have only begun on the atomic energy program. That great force, if properly used by this country of ours, and by the world at large, can become the greatest boon that humanity has ever had. It can create a world which, in my opinion, will be the happiest world that the sun has ever shone upon. [40

Remarks, Pemiscot County Fair
Caruthersville, Missouri
October 7, 1945

•

. . . The same unswerving determination and effort which produced the release of atomic energy can and will enable mankind to live without terror, and to reap untold benefits from this new product of man's genius. [41

Address, Chicago
Army Day
April 6, 1946

. . . **Big Business.** I believe that atomic energy should not be used to fatten the profits of big business. I believe that it should be used to benefit all the people. The largest private corporation in the world is far too small to be entrusted with such power, least of all for its own profit. [42

Statement
Milwaukee, Wisconsin
October 14, 1948

ATOMIC FALL OUT

. . . The dangers of fall-out are a problem for all people everywhere and should not be made a subject of partisan politics. [43

Statement, 1951

ATOMIC WAR

. . . Civilization cannot survive an atomic war. Nothing would be left but a world reduced to rubble. Gone would be man's hope for decency. Gone would be our hope for the greatest age in the history of mankind—an age which I know can harness atomic energy for the welfare of man and not for his destruction. [44

Address, Fordham University
New York City
May 11, 1946

B

BIPARTISANS

. . . I don't like bipartisans. Whenever a fellow tells me he's bipartisan, I know he's going to vote against me. [45

Speech, Kansas City
Quoted in Quote Magazine
January 21, 1962

BROTHERHOOD

. . . The only sure bedrock of human brotherhood is the knowledge that God is the Father of mankind. [46

Address, National Conference of Christians and Jews
Washington, D.C.
November 11, 1949

. . . We can succeed in achieving brotherhood only if we acknowledge that the ideal of brotherhood is something outside or above us, something by which we in our turn will also be judged. [47

Address, National Conference of Christians and Jews
Washington, D.C.
November 11, 1949

BUDGET

. . . **Balanced.** It is a lot better to have a strong national defense than a balanced budget. [48

Statement
February 17, 1957

BUSINESS

. . . **Labor.** Private capital and private management are entitled to adequate reward for efficiency, but business must recognize that its reward results from the employment of the resources of the Nation. Business is a public trust and must adhere to national standards in the conduct of its affairs. These standards include as a minimum the establishment of fair wages and fair employment practices. [49

State of the Union Message
January 21, 1946

BUSINESSMEN

. . . **Politics.** The difficulty with businessmen entering politics, after they have had a successful business career, is that they want to start at the top. [50

Letter to Editor Business Management Magazine
November, 1962

C

CAMPAIGNING

. . . In most of my campaigns, I find it best not to mention my opponent by name because, by doing so, it just gives him a chance to get into the headlines. [51

Statement
Campaigning, 1948

. . . It isn't important who is ahead at one time or another in either an election or a horse race. It's the horse that comes in first at the finish that counts. [52

Statement
October 17, 1948

. . . We can take heart from a comment made by that great American heavyweight champion Joe Louis. In one fight, some time ago, he had a hard time catching up with his opponent. But Joe finally did catch up with him, and he knocked him out. After the fight, this is what Joe said: "Well, he could run away, but he couldn't hide." [53

Address
Convention Hall, Philadelphia
October 6, 1948

CHALLENGE

. . . **Courage.** As in Jackson's time, we Americans must continue to live courageously. We should emulate the valor and the determination of our forefathers—those brave men who conquered the physical frontiers of this vast continent. The modern economic, political and social frontiers, which still confront all of us, offer an even greater challenge to our moral stamina and our intellectual integrity. This challenge also must be met. This victory must be won. I am confident that, with Divine guidance, no problem on earth exists that will not yield to the intelligence, courage, and eternal faith of free men. [54

Address, Jackson Day Dinner
March 23, 1946

CHANGE

. . . For continued success, we must live in the present and work for the future. As we seek to improve the social order, our policies must remain dynamic, ever sensitive to the impact of changing conditions. [55

Address, Jackson Day Dinner
March 23, 1946

. . . The spectacular progress of science in recent years makes these necessities more vivid and urgent. That progress has speeded internal development and has changed world relationships so fast that we must realize the fact of a new era. It is an era in which affairs have become complex and rich in promise. Delicate and intricate relationships, involving us all in countless ways, must be carefully considered. [56

State of the Union Message
January 21, 1946

. . . Our problems of government are chiefly the conflicts of growth and change. They are the ebb and flow of national existence. But despite these, we move toward tomorrow with the conviction that the spirit of our nation is best expressed in the improving standard of American life. [57

Radio Remarks
January 30, 1946

. . . We are living in a time of profound and swiftly moving change. We see colonial peoples moving toward their independence. It is a process that we, as Americans, can understand and sympathize with, since it parallels our own struggle for independence. [58

Presenting the Wendell Willkie Awards for Journalism
February 28, 1947

CHARACTER

. . . A man cannot have character unless he lives within a fundamental system of morals that creates character. [59

Statement
Press Conference, 1950

CHARITY

. . . If we are to respond to our religious heritage, we must be guided by the principle of charity—charity in the biblical sense of love for one's fellow man. This is the greatest virtue, without which other virtues are of little worth. [60

Address, Washington Pilgrimage of American Churchmen, Washington, D. C., September 28, 1951

. . . Only by helping the least fortunate of its members to help themselves, can the human family achieve the decent, satisfying life that is the right of all people. [61

Inaugural Address January 20, 1949

. . . There is a strength in a federation of any sort. We speak of a "helping hand." But a hand, just by itself, can't help anyone. It is dependent upon muscles, nerves, bloodstream, and brain, a federation of services, mutually helpful. [62

Radio Remarks September 30, 1949

CHILDREN

. . . We cannot insulate our children from the uncertainties of the world in which we live or from the impact of the problems which confront us all. What we can do—and what we must do—is to equip them to meet these problems, to do their part in the total effort, and to build up those inner resources of character which are the main strength of the American people. [63

Address, Midcentury White House Conference on Children and Youth December 5, 1950

. . . The basis of mental and moral strength for our children lies in spiritual things. It lies first of all in the home. And next, it lies in the religious and moral influences which are brought to bear on the children. If children have a good home—a home in which they are loved and understood—and if they have good teachers in the first few grades of school, I believe they are well started on the way toward being useful and honorable citizens. [64

Address, Midcentury White House Conference on Children and Youth
December 5, 1950

. . . **Dogs.** Children and dogs are as necessary to the welfare of this country as Wall Street and the railroads. [65

Remarks, National Conference on Family Life
May 6, 1948

. . . **Food.** Nothing is more important in our national life than the welfare of our children, and proper nourishment comes first in attaining this welfare. The well nourished school child is a better student. He is healthier and more alert. He is developing good food habits which will benefit him for the rest of his life. In short, he is a better asset for his country in every way. The school lunch program provides a cooperative means of assuring adequate nutrition for millions of our children who otherwise might be denied this basic need. [66

Statement
October 22, 1946

. . . **Religious Training.** I do not think I am being old-fashioned when I say that children ought to have religious training when they are young, and that they will be happier for it and better for it the rest of their lives. [67

Address, Midcentury White House Conference on Children and Youth
December 5, 1950

CHRISTMAS

. . . **Age.** As you get older, you get tired of doing the same things over and over again, so you think Christmas has changed. It hasn't. It's you who has changed. [68

Statement
December 1955

. . . **Hopes.** Again our thoughts and aspirations and the hopes of future years turn to a little town in the hills of Judea where on a winter's night two thousand years ago the prophecy of Isaiah was fulfilled. Shepherds keeping the watch by night over their flock heard the glad tidings of great joy from the angels of the Lord singing, "Glory to God in the Highest and on Earth, peace, good will toward men." The message of Bethlehem best sums up our hopes tonight. If we as a nation, and the other nations of the world, will accept it, the star of faith will guide us into the place of peace as it did the shepherds on that day of Christ's birth long ago. [69

Address, Lighting of the National Community Christmas Tree
December 24, 1946

CIVIL AUTHORITY

. . . A free society requires the supremacy of the civil rather than the military authority. [70

Address, Milwaukee, Wisconsin
October 14, 1948

CIVIL RIGHTS

. . . I want our Bill of Rights implemented in fact. We have been trying to do this for 150 years. We are making progress, but we are not making progress fast enough. This country could very easily be faced with a situation similar to the one with which it was faced in 1922. That date was impressed on my mind because I was running for my first elective office—county judge of Jackson County—and there was an organization in that county that met on hills and burned crosses and worked behind sheets. There is a tendency in this country for that situation to develop again, unless we do something tangible to prevent it. [71

Remarks, President's Committee
on Civil Rights
January 15, 1947

. . . It is my deep conviction that we have reached a turning point in the long history of our country's efforts to guarantee freedom and equality to all our citizens. Recent events in the United States and abroad have made us realize that it is more important today than ever before to insure that all Americans enjoy these rights. [72

Address, National Association
for the Advancement
of Colored People
June 29, 1947

. . . Men of good will everywhere are striving, under great difficulties, to create a worldwide moral order, firmly established in the life of nations. For us here in America, a new charter of human freedom will be a guide for action; and in the eyes of the world, it will be a declaration of our renewed faith in the American goal—the integrity of the individual human being, sustained by the moral consensus of the whole nation, protected by a government based on equal freedom under just laws. [73

Statement
October 29, 1947

. . . Some of our citizens are still denied equal opportunity for education, for jobs and economic advancement, and for the expression of their views at the polls. Most serious of all, some are denied equal protection under the laws. Whether discrimination is based on race, or creed, or color, or land of origin, it is utterly contrary to American ideals of democracy. [74

State of the Union Message
January 7, 1948

. . . We can no longer afford the luxury of a leisurely attack upon prejudice and discrimination. There is much that state and local governments can do in providing positive safeguards for civil rights. But we cannot any longer await the growth of a will to action in the slowest state or the most backward community. Our national government must show the way. [75

Address, National Association for the Advancement of Colored People
June 29, 1947

. . . We have recently witnessed in this country numerous attacks upon the constitutional rights of individual citizens as a result of racial and religious bigotry. Substantial segments of our people have been prevented from exercising fully their right to participate in the election of public officials, both locally and nationally. Freedom to engage in lawful callings has been denied. The will to fight these crimes should be in the hearts of every one of us. [76

State of the Union Message
January 6, 1947

COLLEGE

. . . A college is an institution that is dedicated to the future. It is based on faith and hope—faith in the basic decency of our fellow men, and hope that the increase of knowledge will promote the general welfare. [77

Address, Wake Forest College
North Carolina
October 15, 1951

COMMON SENSE

. . . **Americans.** I have boundless faith in the common sense and ultimate fairness of the American people. Given unity of purpose and a determination to meet the challenge of the times, there is nothing too difficult for them to accomplish. They have performed miracles during the war. They can, they will, surmount the difficulties which face them now on their road to continued peace and well-being. [78

Radio Address
October 30, 1945

. . . Communism exalts the state and degrades the individual; communism holds that the individual is only a means to an end; communism holds that the duty of the individual is to conform to the state's definition of what is good for him. This we are against. We must resist it, and we must provide aid and hope to those in the world who resist it. But we cannot resist it with our full strength unless we all work for the success of our democracy continually and reaffirm our faith in that democracy. [79

Address, Chicago Swedish Pioneer Centennial Association
June 4, 1948

. . . Communism masquerades as a doctrine of progress. It is nothing of the kind. It is, on the contrary, a movement of reaction. It denies that man is master of his fate, and consequently denies man's right to govern himself. [80

St. Patrick's Day Address
New York City
March 17, 1948

. . . Communism seeks to induce men to surrender their freedom by false promises of a better life. But the great danger of communism does not lie in its false promises. It lies in the fact that it is an instrument of an armed imperialism which seeks to extend its influence by force. [81

Address, Alexandria, Virginia
February 22, 1950

. . . Communism succeeds only when there is weakness, or misery, or despair. [82

Address, Chicago Swedish Pioneer
Centennial Association
June 4, 1948

. . . Communist imperialism preaches peace but practices aggression. [83

Speech
September 1, 1950

. . . The menace of communism lies primarily in those areas of American life where the promise of democracy remains unfulfilled. [84

Address, Chicago Swedish Pioneer
Centennial Association
June 4, 1948

. . . Today communism has become the greatest foe of the free mind. We should be constantly on the alert and vigilant to resist its efforts to infiltrate our society. But in making this flight, we should be sure we do not fall into the trap of adopting the totalitarian tactics of the Communists. [85

Address, Westminster College
Fulton, Missouri
April 1954

. . . You cannot stamp out communism by driving it underground. You can prevent communism by more and better democracy. [86

Address, Chicago Swedish Pioneer Centennial Association
June 4, 1948

. . . **Suffering.** Communism thrives on misery. Human suffering nourishes the Communist menace. That menace withers away where there is prosperity, justice and tolerance. [87

Address, Mechanics Hall
Boston, Mass.
October 27, 1948

COMMUNITY

. . . What is good for some people in a community is good for all. What harms some, harms all. [88

Radio Address
September 26, 1947

CONGRESS

. . . The fact that we have had a Republican Congress for two years has at least given you a chance to see what they are like and what they will do. I call it the worst Congress, except one, this country has ever had. Because I was in the White House, however, they didn't get to walk backwards quite as fast as they wanted to. [89

Informal Remarks
Grand Rapids, Michigan
September 6, 1948

. . . **80th.** Let's take a look at the record of the 80th Congress they're so proud of. I call it the "notorious, do-nothing, Republican 80th Congress." Maybe I ought to leave out the "do-nothing" part of it, because it did do some things—most of them bad. [90

Address, Convention Hall
in Philadelphia
October 6, 1948

. . . **World Situation.** If you tell Congress everything about the world situation, they get hysterical. If you tell them nothing they go fishing. [91

Statement
July 17, 1950

CONSERVATION

. . . Conservation has been practiced for many decades and preached for many more, yet only in recent years has it become plain that we cannot afford to conserve in a haphazard or piecemeal manner. No part of our conservation program can be slighted if we want to make full use of our resources and have full protection against future emergencies. [92

Address, Everglades National
Park
December 6, 1947

. . . **Forestry.** The products of the forests contributed mightily to building this Nation. They will be needed for our continued progress and prosperity. If this country is to be sure of an adequate supply of forest products, it must stop destructive cutting and unwise depletion, and build up timber growth. [93

Statement
April 10, 1947

COOPERATION

. . . Cooperation in peacetime is a hard thing to get. There is no incentive to cooperate like there is in war. Bring anybody here during wartime and you get results from him—he was glad to help the government. Now they are all trying to help themselves, and it's just as hard as hell for the President to get any help. [94

Special Conference
American Society of Newspaper Editors
April 18, 1946

. . . If we cooperate, work, and produce, we can attain a richness of life that will be a credit and a benefit to all of us now living, and a real hope and promise to those who come after us. [95

Statement
August 31, 1946

COURAGE

. . . It takes courage to face a duelist with a pistol and it takes courage to face a British general with an army. But it takes still greater and far higher courage to face friends with a grievance. The bravest thing Andrew Jackson ever did was to stand up and tell his own people to their faces that they were wrong. [96

Address, Raleigh, North Carolina
October 19, 1948

COURTS

. . . The spirit and the meaning of our courts do not lie in the material settings we provide for them, but in the living ideas which they enshrine. [97

Address at the Laying of
the Cornerstone of the New
U. S. Courts Building for
the District of Columbia
June 27, 1950

CRIME

. . . **Children.** I am particularly anxious that we should do everything within our power to protect the minds and hearts of our children from the moral corruption that accompanies organized crime. Our children are our greatest resource, and our greatest asset—the hope of our future, and the future of the world. We must not permit the existence of conditions which cause our children to believe that crime is inevitable and normal. We must teach idealism—honor, ethics, decency, the moral law. We must teach that we should do right because it is right, and not in the hope of any material reward. [98

Address, Attorney General's
Conference on Law Enforcement
Washington, D.C.
February 15, 1950

D

DECISIONS

. . . I never sit on a fence. I am either on one side or another. [99

Remarks, Bellefontaine, Ohio
October 30, 1948

DEGREES

. . . **University.** I have a little hesitation about addressing this august body, shall I say, everybody with degrees emeritus and all the other $40 words that go with an education. The only degree that I ever earned was at George Washington University in Washington, D. C. My daughter went to school there for four years and earned me a degree. [100

Remarks, University of
California
June 12, 1948

. . . A society of self-governing men is more powerful, more enduring, more creative than any other kind of society, however disciplined, however centralized. We know now that the basic proposition of the worth and dignity of man is not a sentimental aspiration or a vain hope or a piece of rhetoric. It is the strongest, most creative force now present in this world. [101

Radio Report
August 9, 1945

. . . By giving tangible expression to the meaning of democracy, we shall widen and strengthen its hold upon the imagination of the world. [102

Address, Governing Board of the Pan American Union
April 15, 1946

. . . Liberty does not make all men perfect nor all society secure. But it has provided more solid progress and happiness and decency for more people than any other pholosophy of government in history. [103

Radio Address After the Signing of the Terms of Unconditional Surrender by Japan
September 1, 1945

. . . There isn't a word in the English language that has been so severely abused during the last ten years as the word democracy. [104

Statement
March 20, 1949

. . . The stronger the voice of a people in the formulation of national policies, the less the danger of aggression. When all governments derive their just powers from the consent of the governed, there will be enduring peace. [105

Independence Day Address
July 4, 1947

. . . **Brotherhood.** Democracy has a spiritual foundation because it is based upon the brotherhood of men. [106

Address, Mexico City
March 3, 1947

. . . **Christianity.** In this great country of ours has been demonstrated the fundamental unity of Christianity and democracy. Under our heritage of freedom for everyone on equal terms, we also share the responsibilities of government. Our support of individual freedom—free speech, free schools, free press, and a free conscience—transcends all our differences. [107

Address, Lighting of the National Community Christmas Tree
December 24, 1946

. . . **Definition.** We know that the maximum freedom and dignity of the individual cannot be attained under a dictatorship. Freedom and dignity of the individual can be attained only under a system of law which protects the rights of individuals, and through a government made up of freely elected representatives of the people. When we have this, we have a democratic government—one that is suited to the democratic way of life. This is a simple, fundamental truth. [108

Address, Mexico City
March 3, 1947

. . . **Faith.** Hitler learned that efficiency without justice is a vain thing. Democracy does not work that way. Democracy is a matter of faith—a faith in the soul of man—a faith in human rights. That is the kind of faith that moves mountains—that's the kind of faith that hurled the Iron Range at the Axis and shook the world at Hiroshima. Faith is much more than efficiency. Faith gives value to all things. Without faith, the people perish. [109

Address, St. Paul, Minnesota
October 13, 1948

. . . **Free Enterprise.** Democratic government has the responsibility to use all its resources to create and maintain conditions under which free competitive enterprise can operate effectively, conditions under which there is an abundance of employment opportunity for those who are able, willing, and seeking to work. [110

Statement
February 20, 1946

. . . **Government.** No government is perfect. One of the chief virtues of a democracy, however, is that its defects are always visible and under democratic processes can be pointed out and corrected. [111

Address to Congress
March 12, 1947

. . . **Unity.** Differing languages and differing cultural backgrounds are not an obstacle to democratic unity. Such differences can provide the basis for a richer and stronger democracy. "Freedom" is a word which is found in every language. "Equality" means more than mere political emancipation. [112

Address, Airport
San Juan, Puerto Rico
February 21, 1948

DEMOCRATS

. . . It is our duty to win if we can—for the simple reason that the principles and programs of the Democratic party are what's best for the United States. [113

Addressing Democratic Rally
in Chicago
September 1953

. . . **Andrew Jackson.** Once upon a time, there were a number of citizens who thought that Andrew Jackson ought to have a suitable coffin. At great expense, they went to Syria and purchased a marble sarcophagus. A sarcophagus, as you know, is a tomb—a big marble coffin with a marble lid. These citizens then shipped this marble box to Washington, which was quite a job as it weighed four or five tons. At last, they thought, a suitable resting place had been provided for Andrew Jackson. Well, the only trouble with the project was that Andrew Jackson wasn't dead. Moreover, he wasn't ready to die. And he did not intend to be hurried to his grave. Courteously but firmly he wrote to these well-meaning citizens, and said, "I must decline the intended honor." And they never did get Old Hickory into that thing. You can still see it, if you're interested, out in front of the Smithsonian Institution. It still sits there. Andy wouldn't even be buried in it. I think that this little story has a moral in it. It is this: Before you offer to bury a good Democrat, you better be sure he is dead. [114

Address, Jefferson-Jackson Day Dinner
February 24, 1949

DEPRESSION

. . . I reject the notion that we must have another depression. I am not referring to minor detours and bumps in the road ahead—these we know we shall have. I am referring to economic collapse and stagnation such as started in 1929. This need not happen again, and must not happen again. [115

Special Message to the Congress
January 8, 1947

DICTATORS

. . . The great weakness of dictatorships is that they enslave the minds and the characters of the people over whom they rule. And the effects of this enslavement are most serious in the case of children. [116

Address
December 5, 1950

DIFFERENCES

. . . Differences between men, and between nations, will

always remain. In fact, if held within reasonable limits, such disagreements are actually wholesome. All progress begins with differences of opinion and moves onward as the differences are adjusted through reason and mutual understanding. [117

Address, United Nations Conference
San Francisco
April 25, 1945

DIGNITY

. . . It is our faith in human dignity that underlies our purposes. It is this faith that keeps us a strong and vital people. This is the hour to rededicate ourselves to the faith in mankind that makes us strong. This is the hour to rededicate ourselves to the faith in God that gives us confidence as we face the challenge of the years ahead. [118

State of the Union Message
January 7, 1948

DIPLOMATS

. . . There is too much nonsense about striped trousers in foreign affairs. Far more influence is exerted at home by the baggy pants of the managing editor than ever is exerted by the striped pants in the State Department. [119

Address, American Society of Newspaper Editors
April 20, 1950

DISPUTES

. . . The essence of our problem is to provide sensible machinery for the settlement of disputes among nations. Without this, peace cannot exist. [120

Address, Conference
San Francisco
April 25, 1945

E

ECONOMY

. . . **False.** Any substantial reduction of the 1948 Budget, as submitted to the Congress, must be clearly understood by the American people as a venture into false economy. To the extent that we countenance any such reduction, we shall weaken our own house by our refusal to keep it in basic repair. At best, this is poor judgment. At worse, it is an invitation to disaster. [121

Address, Jefferson Day Dinner
Washington, D. C.
April 5, 1947

. . . **Interest Rates.** We know from long experience that a drastic rise in interest rates works a hardship on the consuming public. It only benefits the privileged few. [122

Statement
March 1966

. . . **National.** The responsibility of preserving our free enterprise system will continue to rest upon the joint efforts of business, labor, the farmers, and the Government. There must be moderation on the part of business, forbearance on the part of labor, all-out effort on the part of the farmer, and wise guidance and action on the part of the Government. There must be unity of effort and a willingness to cooperate in the achievement of our goal of a strong, stable economy. [123

Address, Associated Press
New York City
April 21, 1947

EDUCATION

. . . Education has been defined as a bulwark against the acids of fascism and communism. [124

Address, Rollins College
Winter Park, Florida
March 8, 1949

. . . Men may be educated for justice, liberty and peace. If peace is to endure, education must establish the moral unity of mankind. [125

Statement
July 30, 1946

. . . Money spent for education is a valuable investment in the future of this country. We should move forward and secure a brighter future for the generations in the coming years that will guide the Nation. There is nothing that could be more important to our country's welfare. [126

Informal Remarks
Havre, Montana
May 12, 1950

. . . We must maintain and expand our schools or we shall surrender our liberties without even fighting for them. [127

Address, Indianapolis
October 15, 1948

. . . Without a strong educational system—free of government control—democracy is crippled. [128

Address, Indianapolis
October 15, 1948

. . . You know that education is one thing that can't be taken away from you. Nobody can rob you of your education, because that is in your head; that is, if you have any head and are capable of holding it. Most of us are capable of holding an education, if we try to get it. [129

Informal Remarks
Oregon
June 11, 1948

. . . **Freedom.** A nation where teachers are free to teach, and young men and women are free to learn, is a strong bulwark against dictatorship. [130

Address, Fordham University
New York City
May 11, 1946

. . . **Need Of.** I want to express appeciation to this orchestra for rendering the things that I think most of, and I want to pay a compliment to that young Mr. Graham who sang here a while ago. He has a lovely voice, and I want to give him the same advice that I gave my daughter. He is 17 years old. You finish that education and get yourself a degree from a standard college—I don't care which one it is—because nobody can take that away from you. Then, if you feel that you want a musical career, go and get it. That is what my baby did. I wouldn't let her start in the musical profession until she had finished her education at George Washington University, and she not only spent 4 years getting herself a degree, she got me one for nothing! [131

Remarks, Dinner in Honor of
Joshua Evans,
Washington, D. C.
January 24, 1951

EISENHOWER, DWIGHT

. . . I like Ike, but not as President. He has gotten mixed up with those damn Republicans and doesn't know which way is up. [132

Statement
October 1956

. . . I like Ike—I like Ike so well I would send him back to the Army if I had a chance. [133

Statement
October 12, 1952

. . . I made a mistake when I said he (Eisenhower) had the capacity to serve ably as President of the United States. [134

Quote Magazine
October 12, 1952

. . . **Campaigning Against.** An uninformed president, fronting for the big-time lobbyists shouldn't be in the White House. That's what they (Republicans) are trying to sell you this year. Don't you buy it. [135

Statement
October 5, 1952

. . . **Cuba.** If former President Eisenhower had understood the Monroe Doctrine, we would not have any trouble in Cuba today. [136

Statement
October 14, 1962

. . . You know, the greatest epitaph in the country is here in Arizona. It's in Tombstone, Arizona, and this epitaph says, "Here lies Jack Williams. He done his damndest." I think that is the greatest epitaph a man could have. Whenever a man does the best he can, then that is all he can do; and that is what your President has been trying to do for the last three years for this country. [137

Informal Campaign Remarks
Winslow, Arizona
June 15, 1948

F

FACTS

. . . **Future.** We must have strong minds, ready to accept facts as they are, and to make bold, new plans based on those facts. [138

Address, Dedication, Grand
Coulee Dam
May 11, 1950

FAITH

. . . Just as an active faith sustained and guided the pioneers in conquering the wilderness, so today an active faith will sustain and guide us as we work for a just peace, freedom for all, and a world where human life is truly held sacred. [139

Radio Address
October 30, 1949

. . . This is an age where faith in one's self, faith in freedom, faith in the kinship of man and God, are more important to our survival than all the mighty armaments of war. [140

Address, Arlington National Cemetery
December 21, 1949

FASCISM . . . All Fascism did not die with Mussolini. Hitler is finished—but the seeds spread by his disordered mind have firm root in too many fanatical brains. It is easier to remove tyrants and destroy concentration camps than it is to kill the ideas which gave them birth and strength. Victory on the battlefield was essential, but it was not enough. For a good peace, a lasting peace, the decent peoples of the earth must remain determined to strike down the evil spirit which has hung over the world for the last decade. [141

Address, San Francisco, Closing Session of the United Nations Conference
June 26, 1945

FATE

. . . **Jefferson; Adams.** John Adams and Thomas Jefferson were political enemies, but they became fast friends. And when they passed away on the same day, the last words of one of them was, "The country is safe. Jefferson still lives." And the last words of the other was, "John Adams will see that things go forward." [142

Informal Remarks
Quincy, Massachusetts
October 28, 1948

FEAR

. . . The worst danger we face is the danger of being paralyzed by doubts and fears. This danger is brought on by those who abandon faith and sneer at hope. It is brought on by those who spread cynicism and distrust and try to blind us to our great chance to do good for all mankind. [143

Address, Wake Forest College
North Carolina
October 15, 1951

FOOTBALL

. . . It's a lot tougher to be a football coach than a President. You've got four years as a President, and they guard you. A coach doesn't have anyone to protect him when things go wrong. [144

Statement
September 19, 1965

FOREIGN AID

. . . We will save nothing if we ignore the needs of other nations now only to find the result is World War III. [145

Statement
April 2, 1950

. . . The dangerous situation with which we are faced in Berlin and many other spots and the even more distressing problems which now exist in Cuba, make it apparent that this is not the time when we can undertake to make drastic cuts in our foreign aid program. [146

Statement
September 30, 1962

. . . We cannot abandon the peoples still in need. To do so would be to replace hope with despair in the hearts of these peoples and thus to undermine the spiritual and economic stability upon which our own hopes for a better world must rest. If we fail to do our part, millions of human beings will be denied the elemental necessities of life. Their strength and recuperative powers, which have been slowly growing, will be undermined. The time, now in sight, when they can once more exist without help and make their contributions to the peace, prosperity and progress of the world, will be indefinitely postponed. [147

Message to Congress
February 21, 1947

FOREIGN POLICY

. . . We shall judge the policy of every nation by whether it advances or obstructs world progress toward peace and we wish our own policy to be judged by the same standard. [148

Commencement Address
University of California
June 12, 1948

. . . Our foreign policy must not be wrecked on the rocks of partisanship. United support of a policy that serves the interests of the Nation as a whole must be our aim. [149

Address, Jefferson Day Dinner
April 5, 1947

. . . The people of the United States may disagree freely and publicly on any question, including that of foreign policy, but the Government of the United States must stand as a unit in its relations with the rest of the world. [150

News Conference
September 20, 1946

. . . **Economics.** We are the giant of the economic world. Whether we like it or not, the future pattern of economic relations depends upon us. The world is waiting and watching to see what we shall do. The choice is ours. We can lead the nations to economic peace or we can plunge them into economic war. [151

Address, Baylor University
March 6, 1947

. . . **Peace.** In the pursuit of peace, there is no single path. We must have a policy to guide our relations with every country in every part of the world. No country is so remote from us that it may not some day be involved in a matter which threatens the peace. Remember that the First World War began in Serbia; that the peace of Versailles was first broken in Manchuria; and that the Second World War began in Poland. Who knows what may happen in the future? Our foreign policy must be universal. [152

Address, Chicago, Army Day
April 6, 1946

FRANCE

. . . France has been experiencing a terrible inferiority complex and is still trying to get over it. [153

Quote Magazine
October 20, 1963

FREEDOM

. . . Freedom is not an easy lesson to each, nor an easy cause to sell, to peoples beset by every kind of privation. They may surrender to the false security offered so temptingly by totalitarian regimes unless we can prove the superiority of democracy. Our case for democracy should be as strong as we can make it. It should rest on practical evidence that we have been able to put our own house in order. [154

Address to NAACP, At the Lincoln Memorial,
Washington, D. C.
June 29, 1947

. . . As a nation we are committed to the principle of freedom because we believe that men are created equal. Freedom is a relationship between equals. [155

Address, Madison, Wisconsin
January 27, 1952

. . . Freedom has never been an abstract idea to us here in the United States. It is real and concrete. It means not only political and civil rights; it means much more. It means a society in which man has a fair chance. It means an opportunity to do useful work. It means the right to an education. It means protection against economic hazards. [156

Address, Independence, Missouri
November 6, 1950

. . . Freedom is still expensive. It still costs money. It still costs blood. It still calls for courage and endurance, not only in soldiers, but in every man and woman who is free and who is determined to remain free. Freedom must be fought for today, just as our fathers had to fight for freedom when the Nation was born. [157

Address, Washington, D. C.
July 4, 1951

. . . There is one thing that Americans value even more than peace. It is freedom. Freedom of worship—freedom of speech—freedom of enterprise. It must be true that the first two of these freedoms are related to the third. For, throughout history, freedom of worship and freedom of speech have been most frequently enjoyed in those societies that have accorded a considerable measure of freedom to individual enterprise. [158

Address, Baylor University
March 6, 1947

. . . In the long run our security and the world's hopes for peace lie not in measures of defense or in the control of weapons, but in the growth and expansion of freedom and self-government. As these ideals are accepted by more and more people, as they give greater meaning and richer content to the lives of millions, they become the greatest force in the world for peace. [159

Address, Alexandria, Virginia
February 22, 1950

. . . In the present anxieties and troubles of the world, the real strength of our country lies not in arms and weapons . . . but in the freedom of our citizens and their faith in a democratic society. [160

Quote Magazine
February 26, 1950

. . . Sometimes we may forget just what freedom means to us. It is as close to us, as important to us, as the air we breathe. Freedom is in our homes, in our schools, in our churches. It is in our work and our Government and the right to vote as we please. [161

Radio and Television Address
December 15, 1950

. . . Steadfast in our faith in the Almighty, we will advance toward a world where man's freedom is secure. To that end we will devote our strength, our resources, and our firmness of resolve. With God's help, the future of mankind will be assured in a world of justice, harmony, and peace. [162

Inaugural Address
January 20, 1949

. . . Until the captive peoples of the world emerge from darkness, they cannot see the hand we hold out in friendship.
[163

Quote Magazine
January 1, 1950

. . . **Peace.** We believe that freedom and peace are essential if men are to live as our Creator intended us to live. It is this faith that has guided us in the past, and it is this faith that will fortify us in the stern days ahead. [164

Radio and Television Address
July 19, 1950

. . . **Personal.** As Americans, we believe that every man should be free to live his life as he wishes. He should be limited only by his responsibility to his fellow countrymen. If this freedom is to be more than a dream, each man must be guaranteed equality of opportunity. The only limit to an American's achievement should be his ability, his industry, and his character. These rewards for his effort should be determined only by those truly relevant qualities. [165

Address, National Association for the Advancement of Colored People
June 29, 1947

FREEDOM OF THOUGHT

. . . In recent years, our enemies have clearly demonstrated the disaster which follows when freedom of thought is no longer tolerated. Honest minds cannot long be regimented without protest. [166

Address, United Nations Conference
April 25, 1945

FREE ENTERPRISE

. . . A system of free enterprise does not automatically work out its own adjustments without our giving thought to the process. [167

Address, Jefferson Day Dinner
Washington, D. C.
April 5, 1947

FUTURE

. . . **Americans.** The plain people of this country found the courage and the strength, the self-discipline, and the mutual respect to fight and to win, with the help of our allies, under God. I doubt if the tasks of the future are more difficult. But if they are, then I say that our strength and our knowledge and our understanding will be equal to those tasks. [168

Message to Congress on State of the Union
January 21, 1946

G

GENERALS

. . . It's the President's privilege to appoint generals—and sometimes to fire them when it's necessary. It's not a pleasant procedure at all. If you look through the history of the country, you'll find that James K. Polk had to do that; Abraham Lincoln had to do it four times, and one of the fellows—after Lincoln had fired him—ran against him for President. It didn't happen in my case! [169

Press Conference
April 27, 1950

GOALS

. . . **Faith.** Our common goal is to arouse and invigorate the faith of men to attain eternal values in our own generation—no matter what obstacles exist or may arise in the path. [170

Exchange of Messages
With Pope Pius XII
August 28, 1947

GOLF

. . . I never had enough money to play golf. [171

Quote Magazine
September 25, 1955

GOOD INTENTIONS

. . . About the meanest thing you can say about a man is that he means well. [172

Address, Pendleton, Oregon
May 10, 1950

GOOD NEIGHBOR POLICY

. . . The good-neighbor policy applies to international relations the same standards of conduct that prevail among self-respecting individuals within a democratic community. It is based upon mutual respect among nations, the respect that each accords to the rights of the other, without distinction of size, wealth, or power. It is an expression of that bond of common belief which we call democracy. It is the only road into the future that will lead us to our goal of universal peace and security. Along that road we shall persevere. [173

Address, Mexico City
March 3, 1947

. . . Our Government is the government of a Republic—delegated powers, diffused powers, legislative powers, executive powers, judicial powers, all separate and independent, which makes it very difficult for an individual to be persecuted under our system. [174

Remarks, Delegates of Boys Nation
August 9, 1946

. . . **Efficiency.** If you want an efficient government, why then go someplace where they have a dictatorship and you'll get it. [175

Lecture series Columbia University
April 28, 1959

. . . **Hope.** There must be life and hope in government. We must achieve and pioneer in the great frontier of human rights and social justice. [176

Address, St. Paul, Minnesota
October 13, 1948

. . . **The People.** The Government is the people. We only represent what we believe to be the opinion of the majority of the people. When I act as President of the United States, when we act as Senators and as Congressmen, we are expressing what we believe to be the views of the majority. [177

Remarks, Delegates of Boys Nation
August 9, 1946

GREED

. . . Selfishness and greed, individual or national, cause most of our troubles. He Whose birth we celebrate tonight (Christmas) was the world's greatest teacher. He said: "Therefore all things whatsoever ye would that men should do to you, do ye even so to them; for this is the law and the prophets." [178

Address, Lighting the National Community Christmas Tree at the White House
December 24, 1946

H

HATE

. . . It is one of the major tragedies of war that the passions it unleashes do not automatically subside with the fighting. They must be subdued gradually. And it usually takes long, patient, and courageous effort. [179

Address, Raleigh, North Carolina
October 19, 1948

HEALTH

. . . Healthy citizens constitute our greatest national resource. In time of peace, as in time of war, our ultimate strength stems from the vigor of our people. The welfare and security of our nation demand that the opportunity for good health be made available to all, regardless of residence, race or economic status. [180

Special Message to Congress
May 19, 1947

. . . We should resolve now that the health of this Nation is a national concern; that financial barriers in the way of attaining health shall be removed; that the health of all its citizens deserves the help of all the Nation. [181

Special Message to Congress
November 19, 1945

HERITAGE

. . . The men and women who made this country great and kept it free were plain people with courage and faith. Let us justify this heritage. [182

Radio Report
January 3, 1946

HISTORIANS

. . . And what I want to say to historians is that any Monday morning quarterback can win a ball game next Monday, but he can't do it on Saturday. [183

Press Conference
April 27, 1952

HOME LIFE

. . . The spiritual welfare of our people of tomorrow is going to depend on the kind of home life which our Nation has today . . . for home life reflects the Nation's life. It must conform to an ever-rising standard. [184

Address, Columbus, Ohio
March 6, 1946

HOOVER, HERBERT

. . . Many of you recall that campaign of 1928, when Al Smith ran for President against that well-known engineer—Herbert

Hoover. He was one engineer who really did a job of running things backward. [185

Address, Mechanics Hall
Boston, Mass.
October 27, 1948

HOPE

. . . Hope has become the secret weapon of the forces of liberation. [186

Address, Joint Session of Congress
April 16, 1945

. . . Aggressors can not dominate the human mind. As long as hope remains, the spirit of man will never be crushed. [187

Address, Joint Session of Congress
April 16, 1945

HOUSING

. . . The Republican leadership wouldn't give the American people the kind of housing they need because the rich real estate lobby opposed it. The Hoover slogan, if you remember, back in 1929 and 1930 was, "Two cars in every garage." The Republican slogan today is, "Two families in every garage."

[188

Remarks, Newark, New Jersey
October 7, 1948

HUMANISM

. . . In our generous impulses we should follow the admonition set forth in St. Matthew's Gospel. Our Lord, bidding us to aid and comfort our stricken neighbor, whoever he may be, spoke words as true today as when He uttered them more than nineteen hundred years ago: "Inasmuch as ye have done it unto one of the least of these my brethren, ye have done it unto me." [189

Radio Address
September 26, 1947

HUMAN RIGHTS

. . . The United States has always had a deep concern for human rights. Religious freedom, free speech, and freedom of thought are cherished realities in our land. Any denial of human rights is a denial of the basic beliefs of democracy and of our regard for the worth of each individual. [190

Message, State of the Union
January 7, 1948

HUNTING

. . . I do not like to hunt animals, and I never have. I do not believe in shooting at anything that cannot shoot back. [191

Statement, 1960

HYPOCRISY

. . . My grandfather used to tell me that whenever you see a fellow go up to the mourners' bench and begin to pray out loud, you'd better go home and lock your smokehouse. [192

Quote Magazine
October 12, 1952

I

IDEAS

. . . You cannot get along in the atomic age with horse-and-buggy ideas. [193

Address, Madison, Wisconsin
January 27, 1952

. . . You cannot stop the spread of an idea by passing a law against it. [194

Address, Chicago, Swedish Pioneer Centennial Association
June 4, 1948

IMMIGRANTS

. . . We should not forget that our Nation was founded by immigrants many of whom fled oppression and persecution. We have thrived on the energy and diversity of many peoples. It is a source of our strength that we number among our people all the major religions, races and national origins. [195

Special Message to Congress
July 7, 1947

IMMIGRATION

. . . Common decency and the fundamental comradeship of all human beings require us to do what lies within our power to see that our established immigration quotas are used in order to reduce human suffering. [196

Statement
December 22, 1945

INDEPENDENCE DAY

. . . This day, the men and woman of our armed forces, and many civilians as well, are celebrating the anniversary of American Independence in other countries throughout the world. Citizens of these other lands will understand what we celebrate and why, for freedom is dear to the hearts of all men everywhere. In other lands, others will join us in honoring our declaration that all men are created equal and are endowed with certain inalienable rights—life, liberty and the pursuit of happiness. [197

Statement
The Fourth of July, 1945

INDIFFERENCE

. . . Great republics of the past always passed away when their peoples became prosperous and fat and lazy, and were not willing to assume their responsibilities. [198

Remarks to the President's Advisory Commission on Universal Training
December 20, 1946

INDUSTRIAL PEACE

. . . Industrial peace between management and labor will have to be achieved—through the process of collective bargaining—with Government assistance but not Government compulsion. This is a problem which is the concern not only of management, labor, and the Government, but also the concern of every one of us. [199

State of the Union Message
January 21, 1946

INJUSTICE

. . . To attempt to correct injustice by disunion is to apply a remedy that is worse than the disease. [200

Address, Raleigh, North Carolina
October 19, 1948

INTERNATIONALISM

. . . No nation on this globe should be more internationally minded than America because it was built by all nations. [201

Speech, Chicago, Illinois
March 17, 1945

INTERNATIONAL ORDER

. . . Our people are united. They have come to a realization of their responsibilities. They are ready to assume their role of leadership. They are determined upon an international order in which peace and freedom shall endure. [202

Address, Baylor University
March 6, 1947

INTERNATIONAL PURPOSE

. . . Our faith is in the betterment of human relations. Our vision is of a better world in which men and nations can live together, respecting one another's rights and cooperating in building a better life for all. Our efforts are made in the belief that men and nations can cooperate, and that there are no international problems which men of good will cannot solve or adjust. [203

Address, Cornerstone Laying
of the United Nations
Building
New York City
October 24, 1949

INTERNATIONAL RELATIONS

. . . International relations have traditionally been compared to a chess game in which each nation tries to outwit and checkmate the other. [204

Address, Mexico City
March 3, 1947

INVOLVEMENT

. . . We have learned, by the costly lesson of two world wars, that what happens beyond our shores determines how we live our own lives. We have learned that, if we want to live in freedom and security, we must work with all the world for freedom and security. [205

Special Message to Congress
November 17, 1947

ISOLATIONISM

. . . Isolationism is a counsel of despair. Isolationism would bring on another war, and it would be a war in which we might stand alone against the rest of the world. [206

Address, Madison, Wisconsin
January 27, 1952

. . . Man has learned long ago, that is is impossible to live unto himself. This same basic principle applies today to nations. We were not isolated during the war. We dare not now become isolated in peace. [207

Address to the United Nations
Conference in San Francisco
April 25, 1945

. . . Isolationism is the road to war. Worse than that, isolationism is the road to defeat in war. [208

Address, St. Louis
June 10, 1950

. . . **Americans.** International problems have moved into the front yard of every American home. No citizen can afford the illusion of being detached from them, for they have created hazards, to his family, his livelihood, and to the security he hopes to build for his children. [209

Quote Magazine
December 19, 1948

J

JAMES, JESSE

. . . He actually was not a bad man at heart. I have studied his life carefully, and I come from his part of the country. James was a modernday Robin Hood. He stole from the rich and gave to the poor, which, in general, is not a bad policy. I am convinced that James would have been an asset to his community, if he had not been diverted into the lawless life. [210

Quote Magazine
March 27, 1949

JEWS

. . . **Europe.** In the trial of war criminals at Nuremberg the fact has been established that 5,700,000 Jews perished under the murderous reign of Hitlerism. That crime will be answered in justice. There are left in Europe 1,500,000 Jews, men, women and children, whom the ordeal has left homeless, hungry, sick, and without assistance. These, too, are victims of the crime of which retribution will be visited upon the guilty. But neither the dictates of justice nor that love of our fellowman which we are bidden to practice will be satisfied until the needs of these sufferers are met. [211

Remarks, Delegation from the
United Jewish Appeal
February 25, 1946

JUSTICE

. . . The friendless, the weak, the victims of prejudice and public excitement are entitled to the same quality of justice and fair play that the rich, the powerful, the well-connected, and the fellow with pull, thinks he can get. [212

Address, Attorney General's
Conference
Washington, D. C.
February 15, 1950

. . . **Peace.** Fortunately, people have retained hope for a durable peace. Thoughtful people have always had faith that ultimately justice must triumph. Past experience surely indicates that, without justice, an enduring peace becomes impossible. [213

Address, Joint Session of Congress
April 16, 1945

. . . **Rights.** Wherever nations of peoples have been overcome by totalitarianism, the practice of justice has been snuffed out. But the ideal remains, deep in the hearts of men. Men will always long for protection against midnight arrest, the slave camp, the torture chamber. Men will never accept these things as right. Today, men feel more deeply than ever that all human beings have rights, and that it is the duty of the government to protect them. [214

Address, Laying of the Corner-stone of the New U. S. Courts Building
District of Columbia
June 27, 1950

. . . **Social Problems.** The solution of the tremendous social problems of our day should not be a partisan affair. No one class, group, or party can hope to solve all the complicated problems facing this Nation. Their solution requires the wholehearted cooperation of every element within our great country. And America will reach its high destiny only if we remain strongly united in the endless quest for justice. [215

Address, Jackson Day Dinner
March 23, 1946

L

LABOR

. . . Labor has its own new peacetime responsibilities. Under our collective bargaining system, which must become progressively more secure, labor attains increasing political as well as economic power, and this, as with all power, means increased responsibility. [220

State of the Union Message
January 21, 1946

. . . The Nation's labor force is its greatest productive asset. Prudent use of our human resources requires a working population, not only large and well-trained but enjoying high American standards of health, education, security, and personal and political freedom. [221

Special Message to Congress
January 8, 1947

. . . Today too many Americans in country clubs and fashionable resorts are repeating, like parrots, the phrase "labor must be kept in its place." It is time that all Americans realized that the place of labor is side by side with the businessman and with the farmer, and not one degree lower. [222

Labor Day Address
Detroit, Michigan
September 6, 1948

. . . **Discrimination.** We must end discrimination in employment or wages against certain classes of workers regardless of their individual abilities. Discrimination against certain racial and religious groups, against workers in late middle age, and against women, not only is repugnant to the principles of our democracy, but often creates artificial "labor shortages" in the midst of labor surplus. [223

Special Message to Congress
January 8, 1947

. . . **Management.** Labor is the best customer management has; and management is the source of labor's livelihood. Both are wholly dependent on each other; and the country in turn is dependent upon both of them. [224

Radio Address
October 30, 1945

. . . **Welfare.** We must now move forward to full achievement of these objectives: useful and remunerative jobs for all; incomes high enough to provide adequate food, clothing and recreation; freedom from unfair competition and domination by monopoly; adequate health protection; more effective social security measures; and educational opportunity for all. [225

Statement
August 31, 1946

LATIN AMERICA

. . . **Unity.** If a realistic view of the world takes full account of the differences that separate nations, it must also take full account of the common beliefs that unite nations. Nowhere is this element of unity—unity of heart and mind—more evident than in the neighborly community of the American Republics. Here we recognize clearly that together we must live and together we must prosper. Therefore, we must have world peace. [226

Address, Mexico City
March 3, 1947

LAW

. . . In our domestic civil life we long ago recognized that the alternative to the rule of the strong was law established by the community. For some years now we have been seeking, with increasing success, to apply this basic concept to international relations. It is no coincidence that the effort to achieve collective world security has been concurrent with the growing acceptance of the Doctrine of Nonintervention. [227

Address, Mexico City
March 3, 1947

LAWS

. . . **Good Government.** Good government requires that a law be administered consistently in all the fields where it is applicable. [228

Special Message to Congress
July 25, 1946

. . . **Justice.** The guilty as well as the innocent are entitled to due process of law. They are entitled to a fair trial. They are entitled to counsel. They are entitled to fair treatment from the police. The law enforcement officer has the same duty as the citizen—indeed, he has a higher duty—to abide by the letter and spirit of our Constitution and laws. [229

Address, Attorney General's Conference
Washington, D. C.
February 15, 1950

. . . **Liberty.** We believe that each individual must have as much liberty for the conduct of his life as is compatible with the rights of others. To put this belief into practice is the essential purpose of our laws. [230

Address, Mexico City
March 3, 1947

LEARNING

. . . In our free society, knowledge and learning are endowed with a public purpose—a noble purpose, close to the heart of democracy. That purpose is to help men and women develop their talents for the benefit of their fellow citizens. Our advance in the natural sciences has led to almost miraculous achievements, but we have less reason to be proud of our progress in developing the capacity among men for cooperative living. In the present critical state of world history, we need, more than ever before, to enlist all our native integrity and industry in the conduct of our common affairs. [231

Commencement Address,
Princeton University
June 17, 1947

LIBERALISM

. . . True liberalism is more than a matter of words. It demands more than sound effects. [232

Address, St. Paul, Minnesota
October 13, 1948

LIBERTY

. . . Events have brought our American democracy to new influence and new responsibilities. They will test our courage, our devotion to duty, and our concept of liberty. But I say to all men, what we have achieved in liberty, we will surpass in greater liberty. [232-a

Inaugural Address
January 20, 1949

. . . We can have confidence in the righteousness of our course. The great ideals of liberty and justice are powerful forces in the hearts of men in every country. The faith in God which sustains us, also sustains men in other lands. Together we can erect an enduring peace. [233

St. Patrick's Day Address
New York City
March 17, 1948

. . . **Vigilance.** Our forefathers came to our rugged shores in search of religious tolerance, political freedom and economic opportunity. For those fundamental rights, they risked their lives. We well know today that such rights can be preserved only by constant vigilance, the eternal price of liberty! [234

Address, Joint Session of Congress
April 16, 1945

LIFE

. . . Human life is something that comes to us from beyond this world, and the purpose of our society is to cherish it and to enable the individual to attain the highest achievement of which he is capable . . . Human life is God-given and infinitely valuable. [235

Remarks
August 9, 1950

. . . Everybody is headed for the same place, and they are headed on the same train, and under the same engineer. [236

Remarks to Members of the
Associated Church Press
Washington, D. C.
March 28, 1951

M

MAN

. . . The only realm in which we aspire to eminence exists in the minds of men, where authority is exercised through the qualities of sincerity, compassion and right conduct. [237

Commencement Address
University of California
June 12, 1948

. . . We do not believe that men exist merely to strengthen the state or to be cogs in an economic machine. [238

Quote Magazine
January 25, 1948

. . . **Individual.** We believe in the dignity of the individual. We believe that the function of the state is to preserve and promote human rights and fundamental freedoms. We believe that the state exists for the benefit of man, not man for the benefit of the state. [239

Address, Mexico City
March 3, 1947

. . . **Rights.** So long as the basic rights of men are denied in any substantial portion of the earth, men everywhere must live in fear of their own rights and their own security. [240

Independence Day Address
July 4, 1947

. . . **The State.** Our American tradition rests on the belief that the state exists for the benefit of man. The American Republics have overwhelmingly rejected the false doctrine that man exists for the benefit of the state. [241

Address, Governing Board,
Pan American Union
April 15, 1946

MANKIND

. . . **Rights.** Every man should have the right to a decent home, the right to an education, the right to adequate medical care, the right to a worthwhile job, the right to an equal share in the making of public decisions through the ballot and the right to a fair trial in a fair court. [242

Quote Magazine
July 6, 1947

MARSHALL PLAN

. . . Emergency aid is no substitute for a long-range recovery program, but it is a vital prerequisite to such a program. If the Western European nations should collapse this winter, as a result of our failure to bridge the gap between their resources and their needs, there would be no chance for them or for us, to look forward to their economic recovery. [243

Quote Magazine
November 23, 1947

MATERIALISM

. . . **Spiritual.** Material things are ashes, if there is no spiritual background for the support of those material things. [244

Remarks, National Convention of the Augustana Lutheran Church
Washington, D. C.
June 7, 1950

McCARTHYISM

. . . McCarthyism: the meaning of the word is the corruption of truth, the abandonment of our historical devotion to fair play. It is the abandonment of "due process" of law. It is the use of the big lie and the unfounded accusation against any citizen in the name of Americanism and security. It is the rise to power of the demogogue who lives on untruth; it is the spread of fear and the destruction of faith in every level of our society . . . This horrible cancer is eating at the vitals of America and it can destroy the great edifice of freedom. [245

Radio and Television Address
Kansas City, Missouri
November 17, 1953

MEDICAL RESEARCH

. . . The Nation's medical research programs must in the future be expanded so that we can learn more about the prevention and cure of disease. The Congress has already recognized this by providing for research into the causes of cancer and mental diseases and abnormalities. Further dividends will accrue to our Nation—and to our people—if research can point the way toward combating and overcoming such major illnesses as arthritis and rheumatic fever, and diseases of the heart, kidneys and arteries. [246

Special Message to Congress
May 19, 1947

MEMOIRS

. . . Sometimes I wish I hadn't undertaken my doggone memoirs. By the time I finish paying taxes, I won't have any profit from them. [247

Quote Magazine
January 31, 1954

MILITARY

. . . **Morale.** It is not the martinets that make an army work, it's the morale that the leaders put into the men that makes an army work. [248

Address, United Nations
General Assembly
October 24, 1950

MINDS

. . . **Knowledge.** Free and inquiring minds, with unlimited access to the sources of knowledge, can be the architects of a peaceful and prosperous world. [249

Commencement Address
Princeton University
June 17, 1947

MINORITIES

. . . **Persecution.** The persecution of minorities goes hand in hand with the destruction of liberty. [250

Address, Chicago Stadium
October 25, 1948

MISERY

. . . Human misery and chaos lead to strife and conquest. Hunger and poverty tempt the strong to prey upon the weak. [251

Special Message to Congress
November 17, 1947

MISSOURI RIVER

. . . The difficulty with the Missouri River is from Sioux City to St. Louis it is a mud river—carries more silt than any other river in the world. Even the Yangtze doesn't carry any more silt than the Missouri. Mark Twain once said that in a wet season you could pour the water of the Missouri from one vessel to the other, if you pushed it and stirred it around enough. [252

Informal Remarks
Peck Dam, Montana
May 13, 1950

MORAL AWAKENING

. . . In our relations abroad and in our economy at home, forces of selfishness and greed and intolerance are again at work. They create situations which call for hard decisions, for forthrightness, for courage and determination. But above everything else, to combat these forces, we call for one thing, without which we are lost. We call for a moral and spiritual awakening in the life of the individual and in the councils of the world. [253

Address, Federal Council
of Churches
March 6, 1946

MORAL CODES

. . . If civilization is to continue, the people of the world must have a moral code by which to live, and on which to act. [254

Statement
December 1956

MORAL FORCE

. . . **United Nations.** The power of the United Nations today is that of moral force. Such force gathers its strength slowly, but it does so surely. [255

Message to Congress
May 22, 1950

MORALS

. . . **Peace.** It would be easy to create a world peace if everybody in the world spoke the same language and read the same newspapers, and had a code of morals based on the necessity for people to live together. Unless we have a code of morals which respects the other fellow's interests, you never can maintain peace. [256

Remarks, Members of the Conference on Emergency Problems in Higher Education
July 11, 1946

MULES

. . . My favorite animal is the mule. He has a lot more horse sense than a horse. He knows when to stop eating. And he knows when to stop working. [257

Press Statement
January, 1952

N

NATIONAL HEALTH

. . . A national health insurance program is a logical extension of the present social security system which is so firmly entrenched in our American democracy. Of the four basic risks to the security of working people and their families—unemployment, old age, death and sickness—we have provided some insurance protection against three. Protection against the fourth—sickness—is the major missing element in our national social insurance program. [258

Special Message to the Congress
May 19, 1947

NATIONAL PARKS

. . . For conservation of the human spirit, we need places such as Everglades National Park where we may be more keenly aware of our Creator's infinitely varied, infinitely beautiful, and infinitely bountiful handiwork. Here we may draw strength and peace of mind from our surroundings. Here we can truly understand what that great Isrealitist Psalmist meant when he sang: "He maketh me to lie down in green pastures, He leadeth me beside still water; He restoreth my soul." [259

Address, Dedication of Everglades National Park
December 6, 1947

NATIONAL PURPOSE

. . . All the questions which now beset us in strikes and wages and working conditions would be so much simpler if men and women were willing to apply the principles of the Golden Rule—"Do as you would be done by." And "Consider the beam in your own eye and pay less attention to the mote in your brother's." [260

Address, Columbus, Ohio
March 6, 1946

. . . America must lead the way to a better world order. We seek increasingly close friendship with all nations. We shall strengthen the foundations of the United Nations. Surely, we shall never retreat merely because of the dangers along the road to peace and progress. Despite opposition and all difficulties, we shall attain our goal—a prosperous and peaceful world. [261

Address, Jackson Day Dinner
March 23, 1946

. . . In the long run that which is best for the Nation is best for all the people. Going forward together in that spirit, we can win a sound and lasting peace-time economy, with high production and prosperity such as this Nation has never known before. [262

Radio Report
October 14, 1946

. . . It is well in this solemn hour that we bow to Washington, Jefferson, Jackson, and Lincoln as we face our destiny with its hopes and fears—its burdens and its responsibilities. Out of the past we shall gather wisdom and inspiration to chart our future course.

With our enemies vanquished we must gird ourselves for the work that lies ahead. Peace has its victories no less hard won than success at arms. We must not fail or falter. We must strive without ceasing to make real the prophecy of Isaiah: "They shall beat their swords into plowshares and their spears into pruning-hooks: nation shall not lift up sword against nation, neither shall they learn war any more."

In this day, whether it be far or near, the kingdom of this world shall become indeed the Kingdom of God and He will reign forever and ever, Lord of Lords and King of Kings. With that message I wish my countrymen a Merry Christmas and joyous days in the New Year. [263

Address, Lighting the National
Community Christmas Tree
at the White House
December 24, 1945

. . . We are determined that every citizen of this Nation shall have an equal right and an equal opportunity to grow in wisdom and in stature and to take his place in the control of his Nation's destiny. We are determined that the productive resources of this Nation shall be used wisely and fully for the benefit of all. We are determined that the democratic faith of our people and the strength of our resources shall contribute their full share to the attainment of enduring peace in the world. [264

Annual Message to the Congress
on the State of the Union
January 7, 1948

. . . On the domestic scene, as well as on the international scene, we must lay a new and better foundation for cooperation. We face a great peacetime venture; the challenging venture of a free enterprise economy making full and effective use of its rich resources and technical advances. [265

State of the Union Message
January 21, 1946

. . . The only expansion we are interested in is the expansion of human freedom and the wider enjoyment of the good things of the earth in all countries. [266

Commencement Address
University of California
June 12, 1948

. . . The strength of our Nation must continue to be used in the interest of all our people rather than a privileged few. It must continue to be used unselfishly in the struggle for world peace and the betterment of mankind and the world over. [267

State of the Union Message
January 5, 1949

. . . We don't want any territory. We don't want to hog the

trade of the world. We *do* want an interchange of ideas and of merchandise and everything of that sort. [268

Remarks
December 20, 1946

NATIONS

. . . **Individuals.** International dealings are no different from those carried on among individuals. Nations represent a community of individuals, and there isn't any more reason why we can't understand each other as nations than why we can't understand each other as individuals. [269

Remarks
July 11, 1946

NATURAL RESOURCES

. . . Resources that occur together in nature must be developed and improved together. [270

Address, Dedication
Grand Coulee Dam
May 11, 1950

NEGOTIATIONS

. . . No single nation can always have its own way, for ours are human problems, and the solution of human problems is to be found in negotiation and mutual adjustment. [271

Address, Cornerstone Laying
United Nations Building
New York, N. Y.
October 24, 1949

NEIGHBORS

. . . **Good.** All will concede that in order to have good

neighbors, we must also be good neighbors. That applies in every field of human endeavor. [272

Address, United Nations Conference
April 25, 1945

. . . **Good.** The Western Hemisphere believes in being good neighbors. I wish all the world could be good neighbors. There isn't any reason why they shouldn't. We ran into two world wars in defense of liberty. We still stand for liberty and the freedom of worship, freedom of conscience and freedom of the individual. [273

Quote Magazine
April 11, 1948

NIXON, RICHARD M.

. . . If he's got any prestige abroad, the country's in a hell of a fix. [274

Quote Magazine
April 17, 1960

. . . You don't set a fox to watching the chickens just because he has a lot of experience in the henhouse. [275

Quote Magazine
October 30, 1960

NOBILITY

. . . **American.** The Constitution declares that there shall be no "titles" of nobility in this Republic. It does not say that there shall be no nobility. We do have what may be described with exact justice as a nobility. But it is not attained by birth. One may come to it from a camp, as Jackson did, or from a university, as Polk did, or from a tailor's bench, as Johnson did. The test is long and brave and honest labor for the country's good. [276

Address, State Capitol
Raleigh, North Carolina
October 19, 1948

NONINTERVENTION

. . . Nonintervention does not and cannot mean indifference to what goes on beyond our own borders. Events in one country may have a profound effect on other countries. The community of nations feels concern at the violation of accepted principles of national behavior by any one of its members. The lawlessness of one nation may threaten the very existence of the law on which all nations depend. [277

Address, Mexico City
March 3, 1947

O

OPTIMISM

. . . I have grown up to look for the good in people. I have never regarded people with suspicion. Such an attitude usually leads to worrying into being a pessimist about everything, people included. [278

Statement
November 1953

P

PACTS

. . . Lasting agreements between allies cannot be imposed by one nation nor can they be reached at the expense of the security, independence or integrity of any nation. [279

Address, Opening of the United Nations General Assembly
October 23, 1946

PAST

. . . **Future.** The past is history. It is the future to which we must now turn our thoughts and our energies. [280

Address, Chicago, Army Day
April 6, 1946

PEACE

. . . For years to come the success of our efforts for a just and lasting peace will depend upon the strength of those who are determined to maintain that peace. We intend to use all our moral influence and all our physical strength to work for that kind of peace. We can ensure such a peace only so long as we remain strong. We must face the fact that peace must be built upon power as well as upon good will and good deeds. [281

Address, Joint Session of Congress
October 23, 1945

. . . Lasting peace requires genuine understanding and active cooperation among the most powerful nations. [282

State of the Union Message
January 21, 1946

. . . Making peace is like repairing the main strands of an intercontinental cable; each strand must be spliced separately and patiently, until the full flow of communication has been restored. [283

Address, San Francisco, Conference on the Japanese Peace Treaty
September 4, 1951

. . . Peace is not a reward that comes automatically to those who cherish it. It must be pursued, unceasingly and unwaveringly, by every means at our command. [284

Address, Chicago, Army Day
April 6, 1946

. . . I have often said, Our goal must be not peace in our time, but peace for all time. [285

Informal Remarks
Galesburg, Illinois
May 8, 1950

. . . Peace is precious to us. It is the way of life we strive for with all the strength and wisdom we possess. But more precious than peace are freedom and justice. We will fight, if fight we must, to keep our freedom and to prevent justice from being destroyed. These are the things that give meaning to our lives, and which we acknowledge to be greater than ourselves. This is our cause—peace, freedom, justice. We will pursue this cause with determination and humility, asking divine guidance that in all we do we may follow the will of God. [286

State of the Union Message
Washington, D. C.
January 8, 1951

. . . Peace is safest in the hands of the people and we can best achieve the goal by doing all we can to place it there. [287

Quote Magazine
July 15, 1951

. . . The benefits of peace, like the crops in the field, come to those who have sown the seeds of peace. [288

Address, Rio de Janeiro
Inter-American Conference
September 2, 1947

. . . We can well afford to pay the price of peace. Our only alternate is to pay the terrible cost of war. [289

Quote Magazine
August 5, 1951

. . . We shall pursue the quest for peace with no less persistence and no less determination than we applied to the quest for military victory. [290

Address, Rio de Janeiro
Inter-American Conference
September 2, 1947

. . . **Christian Principles.** An enduring peace can be built only upon Christian principles. To such a consummation we dedicate all our resources, both spiritual and material, remembering always that "except the Lord build the house, they labor in vain who build it." [291

Exchange of Messages with Pope
Pius XII
August 28, 1947

. . . **Disunity.** We must beware of those who are devoting themselves to sowing the seeds of disunity among our people. The age-old strategy of divide and conquer can be as effective now as it was in the day of the aggressors of old. We must not fall victim to the insidious propaganda that peace can be obtained solely by wanting peace. This theory is advanced in the hope that it will deceive our people and that we will then permit out strength to dwindle because of the false belief that all is well in the world. [292

St. Patrick's Day Address, New York City
March 17, 1948

. . . **Enforcement.** I know that we can get peace in the world if we are in a position to enforce that peace. We wouldn't have peace here in Washington if you didn't have the police around here on the corner. How long do you suppose traffic would stay in line if you didn't have the police lights and the enforcement behind it to make it work? And just how long do you suppose you would have money on your person, if some of our midtown people here found out that there was nobody to keep them from taking it away from you? How far could you walk some night, without having a police force to enforce the law? How far would a court decision go if you didn't have a United States marshall to enforce the court's decision? Do you think John L. Lewis would have paid his fine the other day if he thought there was no enforcement machinery to make him do it? So I am asking for what amounts fundamentally to a police force—in the situation of this country—which will keep peace in the world. [293

President's Special Conference with Editors of Business and Trade Papers
April 23, 1948

. . . **Failure.** There is one pressing reason why we cannot afford failures. When we fail to live together in peace, the failure touches not us alone, but the cause of democracy itself in the whole world. That we must never forget. [294

Remarks, Wendell Willkie
Awards for Journalism
February 28, 1947

. . . **Justice.** Even the support of the strongest nations cannot guarantee a peace unless it is infused with the quality of justice for all nations. [295

State of the Union Message
January 21, 1946

. . . **Strength.** We can fulfill our obligation of service in the cause of peace only by maintaining our strength. The will for peace without the strength for peace is of no avail. [296

Address, Kansas City
June 7, 1947

. . . **United Nations.** After the peace has been made, I am convinced that the United Nations can and will prevent war between nations and remove the fear of war that distracts the peoples of the world and interferes with their progress toward a better life. [297

Address, New York City
Opening Session of the United
Nations General Assembly
October 23, 1926

PEOPLE

. . . **Government.** If people couldn't blow off steam they might explode. Half the fun of being a citizen in this country comes from complaining about the way we run our government—state, federal and local. [298

Quote Magazine
September 16, 1951

PERSONAL

. . . I am now in the army of unemployed *presidents*. But it is a very small army. [299

Quote Magazine
February 1, 1953

. . . Maybe the country would have been better off if I had been a concert pianist. [300

Quote Magazine
July 1, 1962

PERSUASION

. . . The principal power the President has is to bring people in and try to persuade them to do what they ought to do without persuasion. That's what I spent most of my time doing. That's what the powers of the Presidency amount to. [301

Quote Magazine
March 21, 1965

POLITICAL PARTIES

. . . Political parties are the instruments through which democracy works. Our party system remains as one of the massive foundations of our liberty. Only the free play of political opposition can guarantee the survival of civil freedom. [302

Address, Jackson Day Dinner
March 23, 1946

POLITICIANS

. . . **Philosophers.** I don't pretend to be a philosopher. I'm just a politican from Missouri and proud of it. [303

Quote Magazine
October 23, 1955

. . . **Statesmen.** A politician is a man who understands government. Usually, if he understands it well enough and has made a reputation, as he should have, he will wind up—when he is dead—by being called a statesman. You have to have your own definition of what to call things political. It depends altogether on what your viewpoint is. If you are for it, it is statesmanlike. If you are against it, it is purely low politics! [304

News Conference
February 23, 1950

POLITICS

. . . **Enemies.** No conversation is sweeter than that of former political enemies. [305

Statement quoted in Quote Magazine
April 1954

POLLS

. . . These polls that the Republican candidate is putting out are like pills designed to lull the voters into sleeping on Election Day. You might call them sleeping polls. [306

Address, Cleveland Municipal Auditorium
October 26, 1948

POVERTY

. . . The roots of democracy will not draw much nourishment in any nation from a soil of poverty and economic distress. [307

Address, Chicago
April 6, 1946

. . . The only kind of war we seek is the good old fight against man's ancient economies—poverty, disease, hunger and illiteracy. [308

Quote Magazine
June 3, 1951

POWER

. . . **Freedom.** Freedom has flourished where power has been dispersed. It has languished where power has been too highly centralized. [309

Address, Baylor University
March 6, 1947

PREJUDICE

. . . Intelligent men do not hate other men just because their religion may be different, or because their habits and language may be different, or because their national origin or color may be different. [310

Address, Fordham University
New York City
May 11, 1946

. . . Many of our people still suffer the indignity of insult, the narrowing fear of intimidation, and, I regret to say, the threat of physical injury and mob violence. Prejudice and intolerance in which these evils are rooted still exist. The conscience of our

Nation, and the legal machinery which enforces it, have not yet secured to each citizen full freedom from fear. We cannot wait another decade or another generation to remedy these evils. We must work, as never before, to cure them now. The aftermath of war and the desire to keep faith with our Nation's historic principles make the need a pressing one. [311

Address, National Association for the Advancement of Colored People
June 29, 1947

PREPAREDNESS

. . . This is an age when unforeseen attack could come with unprecedented speed. We must be strong enough to defeat, and thus forestall, any such attack. [312

State of the Union Message
January 6, 1947

. . . Weakness on our part would stir fear among the small or weakened nations that we were giving up our world leadership. It would seem to them that we lacked the will to fulfill our pledge to aid free and independent nations to maintain their freedoms, or our commitments to aid in restoring war-torn economies. In such an atmosphere of uncertainty, these nations might not be able to resist the encroachments of totalitarian pressures. We must not let friendly nations go by default. [313

Commencement Address, Princeton University
June 17, 1947

. . . We live in a world in which strength on the part of peace-loving nations is still the greatest deterrent to aggression. World stability can be destroyed when nations with great responsibilities neglect to maintain the means of discharging those responsibilities. [314

State of the Union Message
January 6, 1947

PRESIDENCY

. . . If you don't have a good sense of humor, you're in a hell of a fix when you are President of the United States. [315

Quote Magazine
October 5, 1947

. . . You have to be very careful always to keep that (a sense of humor) in mind when you are President of the United States, because if you don't keep that in mind, you will get a bad case of "Potomac fever," and then you are ruined. You know Woodrow Wilson said that a great many men came to Washington and grew up with their jobs, and a very large number came and just swelled up. [316

Informal Remarks
Salem, Oregon
June 11, 1948

. . . I think you're entitled to see your President and to understand what his policies are and what he is thinking about. It wouldn't make any difference where I went, on what excuse I went, or what I did. It's a political matter so far as the Government of the United States is concerned. The President can't cross the street without creating an incident. But this President likes to create incidents. [317

Informal Remarks
Roseville, California
June 12, 1948

. . . I pinned a medal on General MacArthur the other day, and told him I wished I had a medal like that, and he said that it was my duty to give medals, not to receive them. That is always the way. About all I receive are the bricks. It's a good thing I have got a pretty hard head, or it would have been broken a long time ago. [318

Address, United Nations
General Assembly
New York City
October 24, 1950

. . . I have served my time . . . I don't want to be carried out of the White House in a pine box. [319

Quote Magazine
July 27, 1952

. . . I have done the best I could; the best for the people. I hope it was enough. [320

Quote Magazine
January 25, 1953

. . . It's almost impossible for a man to be President of the United States without learning something. [321

Quote Magazine
August 14, 1948

. . . The presidency is a killing job—a six man job. I know, I've been through. It requires young men—young in physical and mental ability, if not necessarily young in age. [322

Quote Magazine
July 1, 1956

. . . The President spends most of his time kissing people first on one cheek and then on the other in order to get them to do what they ought to do without getting kissed. [323

Remarks, National Planning Association
February 1, 1949

. . . I'm going to run again when I'm ninety. I've announced that a time or two, and you know, some damn fool looked the situation over and said, "When you're ninety, it's an off year," so I can't even run then. I didn't know I was going to stir up all that trouble. [324

Lecture
April 28, 1949

. . . The President is virtually in jail. He goes from his study to his office and from his office to his study, and he has to have guards there all the time. And they do a good job, too—I am not criticizing the guards—but when you get out and see people and find out what people are thinking about, you can do a better job as President of the United States. [325

Rear Platform Remarks
Ohio and Indiana
June 4, 1948

. . . **Criticism.** A President may dismiss the abuse of scoundrels, but to be denounced by honest men honestly outraged is a test of greatness that none but the strongest men can survive. [326

Address, Raleigh, North Carolina
October 19, 1948

. . . **Military Men.** Some of the generals and the admirals and the career men in government look upon the occupant of the White House as only a temporary nuisance who soon will be succeeded by another temporary occupant who won't find out what it is all about for a long time and then it will be too late to do anything about it. [327

Statement 1952

. . . **Qualifications.** First, he should be an honorable man. Then he should be a man who can get elected. Finally, he should be a man who knows what to do after he is elected. [328

Quote Magazine
May 1, 1960

PRESIDENTIAL ELECTION

. . . I had my sandwich and glass of buttermilk, and went to bed at six-thirty. And along about 12 o'clock, I happened to wake up for some reason or other, and the radio was turned on to the National Broadcasting Company. And Mr. Kaltenborn and Mr. Harkness were reporting the situation as it then developed.

Mr. Kaltenborn was saying, "While the President is a million votes ahead of the popular vote, when the country vote comes in Mr. Truman will be defeated by an overwhelming majority."

Mr. Harkness came on, and analyzed the situation as it was then, and as Mr. Kaltenborn had recorded it. And to the sorrow of myself, and to those who were listening with me, it looked very much as if the election would be thrown into the House of Representatives because, of course, it was not possible for me to get a majority of the electoral votes. I went back to bed, and went to sleep.

About 4 o'clock in the morning, the Chief of the Secret Service came in and said, "Mr. President, I think you had better get up and listen to the broadcast. We have been listening all night."

And I said, "All right." I turned the darn thing on, and there was Mr. Kaltenborn again. Mr. Kaltenborn was saying, "While the President has a lead of two million votes, it is certainly necessary that this election shall go into the House of Representatives. He hasn't an opportunity of being elected by a majority of the electoral votes of the Nation!"

And Mr. Harkness came on and analyzed the situation.

I called the Secret Service men in, and I said, "We'd better go back to Kansas City, it looks as if I'm elected!"

Along about 10 o'clock, I had a telegram which said that the election was over, and that I should be congratulated on the fact that I had won the election. Apparently it was too bad, but it happened! [329

Remarks, Dinner of Presidential Electors
January 19, 1949

PRESIDENTS

. . . Some of the Presidents were great and some of them weren't. I can say that, because I wasn't one of the great presidents, but I had a good time trying to be one. [330

Remarks to a Newspaper Man
April 27, 1959

THE PRESS

. . . I am amazed, sometimes, when I find that some of you disagree with me. When I consider how you disagree among yourselves, I am somewhat comforted. I begin to think that maybe I'm all right, after all! [331

Address, American Society of Newspaper Editors
April 17, 1948

. . . I have just been reading a book by a fellow named Pollard, "Presidents and the Press." When you read what the press had to say about Washington, Jefferson, and Lincoln, and the other Presidents, you would think that we never had a decent man in the office since the country began. [332

Special Conference with Editors of Business and Trade Papers
April 23, 1948

. . . The idea of a free press is fundamental to the freedoms that we cherish as Americans. While there are limitations on all our freedoms, including the freedom of the press, we can say without fear of challenge that we have a press that is freer than any other in the world today. Our press in general has outgrown the provincialism, the narrow isolationism, of another era. It is doing a valiant service in educating us to understand that we must live in "one world." [333

Remarks, Presenting the Wendell Willkie Awards for Journalism
February 28, 1947

PRIVATE ENTERPRISE

. . . Our general objective is to move forward to find the way in time of peace to the full utilization and development of our physical and human resources that were demonstrated so effectively in the war. To accomplish this, it is not intended that the Federal Government should do things that can be done as well for the Nation by private enterprise, or by State and local governments. On the contrary, the war has demonstrated how effectively we can organize our productive system and develop the potential abilities of our people by aiding the efforts of private enterprise. [334

Message to Congress
on State of the Union
January 21, 1946

PROBLEMS

. . . **Reality.** We don't propose, like some people, to meet today's problems by saying that they don't exist, and tomorrow's problems by wishing that tomorrow wouldn't come. [335

Address, Kansas City
September 29, 1949

. . . **Solutions.** If men and nations would but live by the precepts of the ancient prophets and the teachings of the Sermon on the Mount, problems which now seem so difficult would soon disappear. [336

Address, Columbus, Ohio
March 6, 1946

PRODUCTION

. . . Production means employment. It means economic

wealth. It means higher wages and lower prices. It means the difference between strength and prosperity on the one hand, and uncertainty and depression on the other. [337

Address, Opening Session,
Labor-Management Conference
November 5, 1945

PROGRESS

. . . All of us want our children to have a better life than we had, and it should be the constant aim of each generation to make things better for the next. It has always been a part of the American dream, and I think we have been successful in accomplishing it to a most remarkable degree. [338

Rear Platform Remarks
Havre, Montana
May 12, 1950

. . . On the foundation of our victory we can build a lasting peace, with greater freedom and security for mankind in our country and throughout the world. We will more certainly do this if we are constantly aware of the fact that we face crucial issues and prepare now to meet them. To achieve success will require both boldness in setting our sights and caution in steering our way on an uncharted course. But we have no luxury of choice. We must move ahead. No return to the past is possible. [339

Message to Congress on State
of the Union
January 21, 1946

PROSPERITY

. . . Prosperity cannot be the concern of one party or of one group. It cannot be attained without the good will and the cooperation of all. [340

Special Message to Congress
January 8, 1947

. . . **Unity.** The farmer, the workingman, and the businessman must prosper together, or they go down together. [341

Address, Omaha, Nebraska
June 5, 1948

PUBLICITY

. . . My grandson was on the front page of newspapers when he was only three days old. It took me fifty years to make it. [342

Quote Magazine
June 23, 1957

PUBLIC SERVICE

. . . The strength of this Republic lies in the fact that so many millions of men and women, who hold no office and aspire to none, recognize as clearly as Presidents Jackson, Polk, and Johnson did that they must serve their country before they serve themselves. [343

Address, Raleigh, North Carolina
October 19, 1948

Q

QUITTERS

. . . When things look difficult, there are always a lot of people who want to quit. We had people like that in the Revolutionary War, and we have had them in every war and every crisis of our history. Thomas Paine called them summer soldiers and sunshine patriots. [344

Address, Philadelphia, Pa.
February 3, 1951

R

REACTIONARIES

. . . The challenge of the 20th century is the challenge of human relations, and not of impersonal natural forces. The real dangers confronting us today have their origins in outmoded habits of thought, in the inertia of human nature, and in preoccupation with supposed national interests to the detriment of the common good. [345

Address, Cornerstone Laying
United Nations Building
New York City
October 24, 1949

. . . The reactionaries hold that government policies should be designed for the special benefit of small groups of people who occupy positions of wealth and influence. Their theory seems to be that if these groups are prosperous, they will pass along some of their prosperity to the rest of us. This can be described as the "trickle down theory." [346

Address, St. Paul, Minnesota
November 3, 1949

. . . Those men who live in the past remind me of a toy I'm sure all of you have seen. The toy is s small wooden bird called the "Floogie Bird." Around the Floogie Bird's neck is a label reading: "I fly backwards. I don't care where I'm going. I just want to see where I've been."

These backward-looking men refuse to see where courageous leadership can take this Nation in the years that lie ahead. These men of small vision and faint hearts have set up their familiar cry, "Of course it's fine, but it can't be done."

How history repeats itself! How familiar all this must sound to those who study the story of Jefferson's Louisiana Purchase, or Jackson's efforts to open up the West!

The men who ridiculed Jefferson and Jackson were men of small courage and big fears. Their political descendants are to be found among those who were afraid to attempt recovery in the 1930's and who are now afraid to make farsighted preparations for American prosperity. [347

Address, Jefferson-Jackson
Day Dinner
February 19, 1948

REASON

. . . **Brotherhood.** When the sages and the scientists, the philosophers and the statesmen, have all exhausted their studies of atomic energy, one solution and only one solution will remain—the substitution of decency and reason and brotherhood for the rule of force in the government of man. [348

Address, Columbus, Ohio
March 6, 1946

RELIGION

. . . Religious faith and religious work must be our reliance as we strive to fulfill our destiny in the world. [349

Radio Address
October 30, 1949

. . . Religion is like freedom. We cannot take it for granted. Man—to be free—must work at it. And man—to be truly religious—must work at that, too. Unless men live by their faith, and practice that faith in their daily lives, religion cannot be a living force in the world today. [350

Radio Address
October 30, 1949

. . . Religion is not an easy thing. It is not simply a comfort to those in trouble or a means of escaping from present difficulties, as some people today would have us believe. Religion is not a negative thing. It is not merely a series of prohibitions against certain actions because they are wicked. Our religion includes these elements. But it also includes much more. It is a positive force that impels us to affirmative action. We are under divine orders—not only to refrain from doing evil, but also to do good and to make this world a better place in which to live. [351

Address, Cornerstone Laying
New York Avenue
Presbyterian Church
Washington, D. C.
April 3, 1951

. . . World Government. We have tried to write into the Charter of the United Nations the essence of religion. The end of aggression, the maintenance of peace, the promotion of social justice and individual rights and freedoms, the substitution of reason and justice for tyranny and war, the protection of the small and weak nations—by these principles the United Nations have laid the framework of the Charter on thhe sound rock of religious principles. [352

Address, Columbus, Ohio
March 6, 1946

RELIGIOUS FREEDOM

. . . We have built our Nation not by trying to wipe out differences in religion, or in tradition, or customs among us, not by attempting to conceal our political and economic conflicts, but instead by holding to a belief which rises above all differences and conflicts.

That belief is that all men are equal before God.

With this belief in our hearts, we can achieve unity without eliminating differences—we can advance the common welfare without harming the dissenting minority.

Just as that belief has enabled us to build a great Nation, so it can serve as the foundation of world peace. [353

Address, Spokane, Washington,
Gonzaga University
May 11, 1950

REPUBLICANS

. . . I have studied the Republican Party for years at close hand, in the capital of the United States. And I have discovered where the Republicans stand on most of the major issues. Since they won't tell you themselves, I am going to tell you:

They approve of the American farmer—but they are willing to help him go broke.

They stand four-square for the American home—but not for housing.

They are strong for labor—but they are stronger for restricting labor's rights.

They favor a minimum wage—the smaller the minimum the better.

They endorse educational opportunity for all—but they won't spend money for teachers or for schools.

They think modern medical care and hospitals are fine—for people who can afford them.

They approve of social security benefits—so much so that they took them away from almost a million people.

They believe in international trade—so much so that they crippled our reciprocal trade program, and killed our International Wheat Agreement.

They favor the admission of displaced persons—but only within shameful racial and religious limitations.

They consider electric power a great blessing—but only when the private power companies get their rake-off.

They say TVA is wonderful—but we ought never to try it again.

They condemn "cruelly high prices"—but fight to the death every effort to bring them down.

They think the American standard of living is a fine thing—so long as it doesn't spread to all the people.

And they admire the Government of the United States so much that they would like to buy it. [354

Address, St. Paul, Minnesota
Municipal Auditorium
October 13, 1948

. . . A sound government to the Republican is the kind of government where the President makes nice sounds while the Vice-President snarls. [355

Quote Magazine
November 2, 1958

. . . But it is important for the people of this country to recognize that time has not changed the fundamental outlook of the Republican Party. The leopard has not changed his spots; he has merely hired some public relations experts. They have taught him to wear sheep's clothing, and to purr sweet nothings about unity in a soothing voice. But it's the same old leopard. [356

Address, Buffalo, New York
October 8, 1948

. . . **Harmony.** The less harmony there is in the Republican Party, the better suited I am. [357

News Conference
July 14, 1949

. . . **Liberal.** I have often wondered what a so-called liberal Republican thinks. On election year they call him out and pat him on the back, and send him around over the country to make speeches in support of a platform that he doesn't believe in—and just as soon as the election is over, they put him back in the doghouse, and he votes with the Democrats for the rest of the time. [358

Remarks, Young
Democrats Dinner
May 14, 1948

RESPECT

. . . **Nations.** The only prize we covet is the respect and good will of our fellow members of the family of nations. [359

Commencement Address
University of California
June 12, 1948

RIGHTS

. . . **Individual.** The most important thing in the Constitution of the United States is that the rights of the individual come first. I am imbued with that idea. I believe that this is a Government of and by and for the people, as Abraham Lincoln said. And as far as I can, as President of the United States, I am trying to implement that theory, not only in the United States but in the world at large. [360

Remarks, Reserve Officers Association
Washington, D. C.
June 28, 1950

ROCKEFELLER, NELSON

. . . He's a very fine man. He did several good things for me when I was President. The only thing I have against him is he's a Republican. [361

Quote Magazine
November 29, 1959

ROOSEVELT, FRANKLIN D.

. . . Time will confirm Franklin Roosevelt's outstanding place in history. It is not for me or for any of his contemporaries to attempt to measure his great stature or to estimate the impact of his words and his deeds upon the days of his years. Today, as I think back to my visit to his grave a year ago, it is uppermost in my mind that he was a great humanitarian—that he brought hope and courage to despairing hearts when fear was destroying the faith of the people—and that through the most terrible war in history he remained the symbol of fortitude, justice, and humanity. [362

Remarks, Franklin D. Roosevelt Memorial Program
April 12, 1947

. . . It is with a heavy heart that I stand before you, my friends and colleagues, in the Congress of the United States.

Only yesterday, we laid to rest the mortal remains of our beloved President, Franklin Delano Roosevelt. At a time like this, words are inadequate. The most eloquent tribute would be a reverent silence.

Yet, in this decisive hour, when world events are moving so rapidly, our silence might be misunderstood and might give comfort to our enemies.

In His infinite wisdom, Almighty God has seen fit to take from us a great man who loved, and was beloved, by all humanity.

No man could possibly fill the tremendous void left by the passing of that noble soul. No words can ease the aching hearts of untold millions of every race, creed, and color. The world knows it has lost a heroic champion of justice and freedom. [363

Address before Joint Session
of Congress
April 16, 1945

RUSSIA

. . . What the world needs in order to regain a sense of security is an end to Soviet obstruction and aggression. [364

Commencement Address
University of California
June 12, 1948

S

SCIENCE

. . . National security and the development of the domestic economy depend upon the extension of fundamental scientific knowledge and the application of basic principles to the development of new techniques and processes. [364-a

Statement
October 17, 1946

SECURITY

. . . **World.** We have a higher duty and a greater responsibility than the attainment of our own national security. Our goal is collective security for all mankind. [365

State of the Union Message
January 6, 1947

SELF-DETERMINATION

. . . I believe that we must assist free peoples to work out their own destinies in their own way. [366

Special Message to Congress
March 12, 1947

SELF-RELIANCE

. . . Individual self-reliance and independence of spirit are the greatest sources of strength in this democracy of ours. They mark the difference between free countries and dictatorships. [367

Address, Midcentury White House Conference on Children and Youth
December 5, 1950

SENATE

. . . **Senators.** There was an old county judge who·was with me on the county court in Jackson County, who was a nephew of Senator Money from Mississippi, who had been here in Washington with Senator Money, and who was a very great philosopher. And he gave me some advice before I left Independence to come to Washington. He said, "Harry, don't you go to the Senate with an inferiority complex. You sit there about six months, and you wonder how you got there. And after that you wonder how the rest of them got there." [368

Remarks to Group of New Democratic Senators and Representatives
April 6, 1949

. . . **Senators.** The Senate is always entitled to conversation.

That's one of the reasons for the existence of the Senate. That's the only legislative body left in the world with unlimited debate, and under no circumstances would I limit that debate. I have been a Senator, and I know what it means for a Senator not to be able to say what he pleases. [369

News Conference
December 12, 1945

SKEPTICISM

. . . The immediate, the greatest threat to us is the threat of disillusionment, the danger of insidious skepticism—a loss of faith in the effectiveness of international cooperation. Such a loss of faith would be dangerous at any time. In an atomic age it would be nothing short of disastrous. [370

Address, Navy Day Celebration
New York City
October 27, 1945

SOCIETIES

. . . **Good-Evil.** The ills of society spread like a contagion and no one is safe. But we may take hope in the fact that the good in society is also contagious. [371

Radio Address Opening National Community Chest Campaign
September 26, 1947

SPECIAL INTERESTS

. . . It is easy to be misled by a small group of special interests engaged in a campaign of misrepresentation. We must not let the selfish demands of special groups blind us to the common good. [372

Address, Jefferson-Jackson Day Dinner
February 24, 1949

SPENDING

. . . You cannot balance, as if on scales, the desirability of spending a few billion dollars against the desirability of surviving as a free nation. We must spend to protect ourselves against a menace that threatens to wipe out our civilization. [373

Quote Magazine
July 5, 1953

SPIRITUAL VALUES

. . . The last five years have produced many awesome discoveries in material things. But it has been truthfully said that the greatest discoveries of the future will be in the realm of the spirit. There is no problem on this earth tough enough to withstand the flame of a genuine renewal of religious faith. And some of the problems of today will yield to nothing less than that kind of revival. [374

Address, Conference of Federal Council of Churches
March 6, 1946

STALIN, JOSEPH

. . . I invited Stalin to come to Washington, and he said,

"God willing, I will come." Well, I haven't met anybody yet who believes me, but that is what he said to me. [375

Special Conference with Editors
of Business and Trade Papers
April 23, 1948

STATESMEN

. . . I have an old definition for a statesman, a very old one: A statesman is a dead politician. [376

Remarks, Buffet Supper for
Democratic Members of
Congress
Washington, D. C.
January 11, 1951

. . . I am not an elder stateman. I hate elder statesmen. I am a Democrat and a politican and I'm proud of it. [377

Quote Magazine
April 15, 1956

STRENGTH

. . . **Spiritual.** The basic source of our strength is spiritual. For we are a people with a faith. We believe in the dignity of man. We believe that he was created in the image of the Father of us all. We do not believe that men exist merely to strengthen the state or to be cogs in the economic machines. We do believe that governments are created to serve the people and that economic systems exist to minister to their wants. We have a profound devotion to the welfare and rights of the individual as a human being. [378

Annual Message to Congress on the State of the Union
January 7, 1948

STRIFE

. . . Sometimes the struggle for something that is worth while makes it all the better, after you get it. [379

Remarks, Conference on Education
July 11, 1946

SUMMIT CONFERENCES

. . . I don't believe in them. They don't amount to a damn. I have been to two of them, and nothing was accomplished. [380

Quote Magazine
November 4, 1962

T

TELEVISION

. . . I've got other things to do besides watch television. I never look at it unless my daughter is on it. [381

News Conference
March 29, 1951

TIMIDITY

. . . Stable world relationships require full production and full employment in the United States. There are voices of defeat, dismay, timidity among us who say it cannot be done. These I challenge. They will not guide us to success, these men of little faith. [382

Radio Report
January 3, 1946

. . . We cannot shirk our leadership in the postwar world. The problems of our economy will not be solved by timid men, mistrustful of each other. [383

Radio Report to American People
January 3, 1946

TOLERANCE

. . . Let us determine to carry on in a spirit of tolerance, and understanding for all men and for all nations—in the spirit of God and religious unity. [384

Address, Columbus, Ohio
March 6, 1946

TOTALITARIANISM

. . . The seeds of totalitarian regimes are nurtured by misery and want. They spread and grow in the evil soil of poverty and strife. They reach their full growth when the hope of a people for a better life has died. [385

Special Message to the Congress
March 12, 1947

TRUMAN, BESS

. . . You know, I went to Sunday school right across there—the first time in my life, a long, long time ago, and in that Sunday school class I met a little, blue-eyed, golden-haired girl—my first sweetheart. Her eyes are still blue, but her hair is no longer golden; it's silver—like mine. And she is still my sweetheart. [386

Address, Dedication of the Liberty Bell
Independence, Missouri
November 6, 1950

TRUTH

. . . Intense feeling too often obscures the truth. [387

Address, Raleigh, North Carolina
October 19, 1948

TYRANNY

. . . Tyranny has, throughout history, assumed many disguises, and has relied on many false philosophies to justify its attack on human freedom. [388

St. Patrick's Day Address
New York City
March 17, 1948

. . . Victorious nations cannot, on the surrender of a vicious and dangerous enemy, turn their backs and go home. Wars are different from baseball games where, at the end of the game, the teams get dressed and leave the park. In wars, the victors must make sure that there will not be a recurrence of enemy aggression and tyranny. Tyranny must be rooted out from the very soul of the enemy nation before we can say that the war is really won. [389

Address, Chicago, on Army Day
April 6, 1946

U

UN-AMERICAN ACTIVITIES COMMITTEE

. . . I have said many a time that I think the House Un-American Activities Committee in the House of Representatives was the most un-American thing in America. [390

Lecture Series
Columbia University
April 29, 1959

UNDERSTANDING

. . . As we gain increasing understanding of man, comparable to our increasing understanding of matter, we shall develop, with God's grace, the ability of nations to work together and live together in lasting peace. [391

Commencement Address
Princeton University
June 17, 1947

. . . It is understanding that gives us an ability to have peace. When we understand the other fellow's viewpoint, and he understands ours, then we can sit down and work out our differences.

If there is no understanding, there can be no peace. If we can exchange educators with all the countries in the world, and show our viewpoint, it won't be long before we have a world situation in which we don't have any insoluble difficulties because we will understand each other. [392

Remarks to Members of the
U. S. National Commission
for UNESCO
September 25, 1946

UNITED NATIONS

. . . Our country has taken a leading part in building the United Nations, in setting up its councils, its committees and commissions, and in putting them to work. We are doing everything within our power to foster international cooperation. We have dedicated ourselves to its success. This is not and it must never be, the policy of a single administration or a single party. It is the policy of all the people of the United States. We, in America, are unanimous in our determination to prevent another war. [393

Address, Baylor University
March 6, 1947

. . . It was the hope of the U. N. Charter that helped sustain the courage of stricken peoples through the darkest days of the war. For it is a declaration of great faith by the nations of the earth—faith that war is not inevitable, faith that peace can be maintained.

If we had had this Charter a few years ago—and above all, the will to use it— millions now dead would be alive. If we should falter in the future in our will to use it, millions now living will surely die.

It has already been said by many that this is only a first step to a lasting peace. That is true. The important thing is that all our thinking and all our actions be based on the realization that it is in fact only a first step. Let us all have it firmly in mind that we start today from a good beginning and, with our eye always on the final objective, let us march forward. [394

Address, Closing Session of the United Nations Conference
June 26, 1945

. . . Our hopes for peace based on justice and international cooperation are embodied in the United Nations. We shall continue every effort to attain the ideal of a United Nations which can banish war for all time. [395

Address, Kansas City, Mo.
June 7, 1947

. . . Our ultimate security requires more than a process of consultation and compromise. It requires that we begin now to develop the United Nations Organization as the representative of the world as one society. The United Nations Organization, if we have the will adequately to staff it and to make it work as it should, will provide a great voice to speak constantly and responsibly in terms of world collaboration and world well-being. [396

Message to Congress, State of the Union
January 21, 1946

. . . The American people look upon the United Nations not as a temporary expedient but as a permanent partnership—a partnership among the peoples of the world for their common peace and common well-being. [397

Address, New York City, Opening Session of the United Nations General Assembly
October 23, 1946

. . . The question is how justice among nations is best achieved. We know from day to day experience that the chance for a just solution is immeasurably increased when everyone directly interested is given a voice. That does not mean that each must enjoy an equal voice, but it does mean that each must be heard. [398

Message to the Congress, State of the Union
January 21, 1946

. . . The effectiveness of the United Nations depends upon the Member States meeting all their obligations. Assurance that these obligations will be met depends in turn upon the will of the peoples of the Member States. The vigor of the United Nations stems therefore from a public opinion educated to understand its problems. [399

Remarks Broadcast on the Second Anniversary of the United Nations
June 26, 1947

. . . The United Nations is a mirror in which the state of world affairs is reflected. [400

Message to the Congress
May 22, 1950

. . . Faith without works is dead. We must make our devotion to the ideals of the Charter as strong as the steel in this building. We must pursue the objectives of the Charter with resolution as firm as the rock on which this building rests. We must conduct our affairs foursquare with the Charter, in terms as true as this cornerstone. If we do these things, the United Nations will endure and will bring the blessing of peace and well-being to all mankind. [401

Address, Cornerstone Laying
of the United Nations Building
New York City
October 24, 1949

. . . **Human Rights.** The promotion and protection of basic human rights for all peoples is a fundamental purpose of the United Nations. Active support for the wider realization of these rights and freedoms has been and should continue to be a primary objective of United States policy in the United Nations. [402

Message to Congress
February 5, 1947

. . . **World Justice.** By their own example the strong nations of the world should lead the way to international justice. That principle of justice is the foundation stone of this Charter (the U. N. Charter). That principle of justice is the guiding spirit by which it must be carried out—not by words alone but by continued concrete acts of good will. There is a time for making plans—and there is a time for action. The time for action is now! Let us, therefore, each in his own nation and according to its own way, seek immediate approval of this Charter—and make it a living thing. [403

Address, Closing Session of the United Nations Conference
June 26, 1945

UNITY

. . . We are a people who worship God in different ways. But we are all bound together in a single unity—the unity of individual freedom in a democracy. [404

Address, Conference of the Federal Council of Churches
March 6, 1946

. . . **God.** The unity of our country is a unity under God. It is a unity in freedom, for the service of God is perfect freedom. [405

Address, Philadelphia, Pa.
February 3, 1951

V

VALUES

. . . **Spiritual.** I fear we are too much concerned with material things to remember that our real strength lies in spiritual values. I doubt whether there is in this troubled world today, when nations are divided by jealousy and suspicion, a single problem that could not be solved if approached in the spirit of the Sermon on the Mount. [406

Address, Fordham University
May 11, 1946

VICTORY

. . . Any man who sees Europe now must realize that victory in a great war is not something you win once and for all, like victory in a ball game. Victory in a great war is something that must be won and kept won. It can be lost after you have won it—if you are careless or negligent or indifferent. [407

Radio Report to the American People
on the Potsdam Conference
August 9, 1945

VISION

. . . The American people cannot afford to trust their future to men of little vision. The Bible warns us that where there is no vision the people perish. [408

Address, Chicago Stadium
October 25, 1948

VOTERS

. . . **Voting.** It is not the hand that signs the laws that holds the destiny of America. It is the hand that casts the ballot. [409

Address, Raleigh, North Carolina
October 19, 1948

VOTING

. . . A vote is the best way of getting the kind of country and the kind of world you want. [410

Quote Magazine
October 10, 1948

W

WAR

. . . For us, war is not inevitable. We do not believe that there are blind tides of history which sweep men one way or another. In our own time we have seen brave men overcome obstacles that seemed overwhelming. Men with courage and vision can still determine their own destiny. They can choose slavery or freedom—war or peace. [411

Address, Signing of the
North Atlantic Treaty
Washington, D. C.
April 4, 1949

. . . Ignorance and its handmaidens, prejudice, intolerance, suspicion of our fellow man, breed dictators and breed wars. [412

Address, Fordham University
New York City
May 11, 1946

. . . We have learned the hard way that peace is best at home and abroad with our neighbors. We have fought two world wars within a generation. We have found that the victor loses in total war as well as the vanquished. [413

Address, Mexico City
March 3, 1947

. . . **Abolition.** The only security for the United States, or for any other nation, when the alternative to peace is death and destruction, lies in the abolition of war. [414

Address, Kansas City
June 7, 1947

. . . **Economic Ills.** The danger of war will never be completely wiped out until the economic ills which constitute the roots of war are eliminated. [415

Address, Governing Board of the Pan American Union
April 15, 1946

. . . **Peace.** I don't believe in peace at any price—no honest man does. But I don't believe that because peace is difficult that war is inevitable. [416

Rear Platform Remarks
Elkhart, Indiana
October 26, 1948

. . . **Peace.** It only takes one nation to make war. But it takes two or more to make a peace. [417

Remarks, Hartford, Connecticut
October 27, 1948

. . . With ever-increasing brutality and destruction, modern warfare, if unchecked, would ultimately crush all civilization. We still have a choice between the alternatives; the continuation of international chaos—or the establishment of a world organization for the enforcement of peace. [418

Address, United Nation Conference, San Francisco, California
April 25, 1945

WEALTH

. . . Our national wealth and income are now being redistributed in reverse—from the poor to the rich. [419

Quote Magazine
February 14, 1954

WELFARE

. . . There is room for everybody in this world, and room enough for everybody to have peace, and to have enough to eat, and a place to sleep. [420

Remarks, National Conference on Family Life
May 6, 1948

WISDOM

. . . Wisdom is not the monopoly of strength or size. Small nations can contribute equally with the large nations toward bringing constructive thought and wise judgement to bear upon the formation of collective policy. [421

Address, New York City, Opening Session of the United Nations General Assembly
October 23, 1946

WOMEN

. . . The moral force of women has always had a wholesome influence upon the character of our civilization. They are deeply responsive to the fundamental human values. Women care more for people than for dollars, more for healthy children than fat dividends. Women want a society in which we build schools instead of prisons. Women want a world in which we sow and harvest the seeds of a good life instead of the seeds of war. [422

Address
October 8, 1947

WORK

. . . It is time that every American recognize what our fathers knew—that it is an honorable thing to work with your hands. [423

Labor Day Address,
Cadillac Square, Detroit
September 6, 1948

WORLD CONDITIONS

. . . Memories are short, and appetites for power and glory are insatiable. Old tyrants depart. New ones take their places. Old differences are composed, new differences arise. Old allies become the foe. The recent enemy becomes the friend. It is all very baffling and trying . . . but . . . we cannot lose hope, we cannot despair. For it is all too obvious that if we do not abolish war on this earth, then surely, one day, war will abolish us from the earth. [424

Quote Magazine
September 1965

. . . It's bound to be improving or it would have blown up long ago. [425

Statement
July 1965

WORLD COURT

. . . I am anxious to bring home to you that the world is no longer country-size, no longer state-size, no longer nation-size. It is one world, as Willkie said. It is a world in which we must all get along. It will be just as easy for nations to get along in a republic of the world as it is for us to get along in the republic of the United States. Now, if Kansas and Colorado have a quarrel over a watershed they don't call out the National Guard of each State and go to war over it. They bring suit in the Supreme Court and abide by its decision. There isn't a reason in the world why we can't do that internationally. [426

Remarks, University of Kansas City
June 28, 1945

WORLD LAW

. . . We cannot have lasting peace unless a genuine rule of world law is established and enforced. [427

Message to Congress
February 5, 1947

WORLD LEADERSHIP

. . . The free peoples of the world look to us for support in maintaining their freedoms. If we falter in our leadership, we may endanger the peace of the world—and we shall surely endanger the welfare of this Nation. Great responsibilities have been placed upon us by the swift movement of events. [428

Special Message to Congress
March 12, 1947

WORLD POLICE FORCE

. . . The function of the United Nations is to quench the flames wherever they may break out; to watch throughout the world and extinguish every spark that comes from a difference between governments; to do this, if possible, through the machinery of peaceful arbitration, but to do it in any case. This is so, even if armed conflict must be prevented by the use of an international police force. [429

Address, Jefferson Day Dinner
Washington, D. C.
April 5, 1947

WORLD TRADE

. . . Only through participation in the trade of the world can a country raise its own standards of living and contribute to the welfare of other nations. [430

Address, Little Rock, Dedication of the World War Memorial Park
June 11, 1949

. . . **Free Enterprise.** The pattern of international trade that is most conducive to freedom of enterprise is one in which the major decisions are made, not by governments, but by private buyers and sellers, under conditions of active competition, and with proper safeguards against the establishment of monopolies and cartels. Under such a system, buyers make their purchases, and sellers make their sales, at whatever time and place and in whatever quantities they choose, relying for guidance on whatever price the market may afford. Goods move from country to country in response to economic opportunities. Governments may impose tariffs, but they do not dictate the quantity of trade, the sources of imports, or the destination of exports. Individual transactions are a matter of private choice.

This is the essence of free enterprise. [431

Address, Baylor University
March 6, 1947

WORLD UNITY

. . . We must recognize that the march of events has joined the peoples of the world together, in a common destiny, whether we like it or not. [432

Address, Madison, Wisconsin
January 27, 1952

. . . I am sorry to say all is not harmony in the world today. We have found that it is easier for men to die together on the field of battle than it is for them to live together at home in peace. But those who died have died in vain if in some measure, at least, we shall not preserve for the peace that spiritual unity in which we won the war. [433

Address, Lighting the National Community Christmas Tree at the White House
December 24, 1946

Y

YOUTH

. . . Our young people k . . . The younger generation of today yearns for moral uplift. To the parents of the Nation—and to you of the Churches of God—has come the responsibility of helping them on to the right path. We must help them on the right path. That is the greatest job you can do for America today. [434

Address, Columbus, Ohio,
Conference of the Federal Council of Churches
March 6, 1946

. . . Just keep up the good work. I am perfectly willing to turn the country over to you when your time comes. [435

Address to Boys Attending American Legion Forum in Washington; quoted in Quote Magazine
August 31, 1947

. . . Our young people know a good deal more about everything than the people who are criticizing them. [436

Quote Magazine
December 6, 1959

INDEX